This career choice has the allure of a great social life, a party atmosphere and at all times access to food, drink and friends. Linda Hepworth thought it sounded like fun and has been in the business for more than forty years. She is the author of *If These Tables Could Talk*, a collection of memoirs. This is her second book in which she gives you a few tips on what you might expect day in and day out if you select this career.

Turning the Tables will guide you along the pathway of the entire dining experience. Delicious food, wacky customers and unfortunate mishaps await the reader, as well as unforgettable twists of fate. These stories come from Linda's personal experiences, as well as from stories told to her. You never know who you'll meet or what can happen in this line of work. These sometimes outrageous tales describe what can go wrong, but also what is appealing and ultimately rewarding about the restaurant business.

Turning the Tables

by Linda Hepworth

To Joanne –
 Best wishes –

Edited by Carol Callahan

Linda Hepworth

ACKNOWLEDGEMENTS

I would like to thank many friends who helped me with these stories, starting with Mary "Futon" Hughes for her encouragement, and my editor, Carol Callahan, who magically transformed my ideas into a coherent book. Special thanks go to my better half, Thor, for his love, patience, suggestions and positive reinforcement for my project.

Thanks go to my Mom and my whole family for their good ideas, editing tips and for the wonderful trip to Italy in 2001 with Jeri, Tracy and Jodie, my "*tre sorelli*" and Deborah, my "*bella sorella*." We had three weeks of dining out, wine with every meal and long conversations. Mom was correct in saying we would remember it for the rest of our lives.

Some of those who contributed with their help and restaurant stories of their own are, in no particular order, Sherry Julin, Denise Parker, Marlene McIver, Erin Whitt, Julia Fornage, Michelle Hartwell, Cindy Duncan Gutierrez, Mark Boynton, Mike Queirolo, Claudia and Bill Young, Bev and Mignon, Ed and Bette Hegeman, Suzanne and Pat Ryan, Jim Kidder, Bill Maley, Bill and Marge Turner, Marge Kenyon and Deborah Beal. I want to thank my photographers, Deborah Hepworth and Christine Minhondo. If I've overlooked any of my contributors, please accept my apologies.

Desmond Lee and Carl Jukkola told me many of their own interesting dining experiences and kept my cupboards full of chocolate to facilitate my writing. I want to thank Daniel Tierney for his enthusiasm, Paula Helene Beard for keeping the books and Roger Minhondo, owner of *Le Chalet Basque*, for allowing me to perform as an author as well as a waitress.

Marie-Hélène Azcona Perreault
October 21, 1960 – June 30, 2012

She was a gracious and generous friend, a loving wife
and a bartender extraordinaire; suddenly called home
in the middle of her shift.
We will always remember our Mary Ellen.

ISBN 13: 978-1480205031
ISBN 10: 1480205036

Photo credits:
Wikimedia Commons: Cover: Silvia Planas; pg. 1: Dorina Andress; pg. 3: Veronidae; pg. 23: Jorge Royan; pg. 29: J. Smith; pg. 35: COD Newsroom; pg. 36: Ben Schumin; pg. 39: Bobak Ha'eri; pg. 45: Luigi Novi; pg. 47: Bangin; pg. 52: Harlequeen; pg. 55: Ignis; pg. 63: Herrick; pg. 66: Brosen; pg. 71: Cyclonebill; pg. 78: Funpika; pg. 79: AlMare; pg. 81: tomas er; pg. 82: Dennis Mojado; pg. 95: Kelly Kaneshiro; pg. 96: David Yu Photography. Licensed from Bigstock; pg. 4, 6, 9, 12, 24, 31, 34, 41, 53, 56, 62, 100, 103 & 105. www.rodjonesphotography.co.uk; pg. 18. Phil Frank; pg. 62. Christine Minhondo; pg. 105. Public domain; pgs. 2, 11, 14, 21, 33, 37, 40, 49, 59, 64, 73, 74, 77, 85, 99 & 101.

Printed in the United States

TABLE OF CONTENTS

This book is dedicated to the goal of providing excellent customer service.

CHAPTER ONE

IT'S ALL ABOUT THE FOOD

"All restaurants should have the servers
taste the food."

I love food. Serving in restaurants is the right career choice for me because I can talk about food for a living.

At work one day, I was sharing recipes with a friend of mine. He is Italian, likes to cook and often tells us of the fantastic dinners he prepares. In many cases, they are his mother's recipes and he's proud of them. We were discussing shellfish and I told him that generally speaking, fish is not my favorite. He pressed me to take his recipe for cioppino. "Everybody likes cioppino," he said, "It's full of shellfish, tomatoes, garlic; how could you not like it?" He had the recipe typed out, handed it to me proudly and told me to tell him when I made it.

When I got home, I glanced at the recipe. As expected, clams, mussels, white fish and shrimp topped the list. Also included were tomatoes, garlic, onions and basil for seasoning. After that, there was an ingredient listed that I had never seen before. The recipe called for three dozen "pig nipples." What? I read it again; it indeed said "pig nipples."

I was fortunate to work with a Swiss chef for my second job and I was heading there that evening. He would know what this is, I thought to myself, and carried the recipe to work with me to show him the list. Pig nipples? I didn't want to sound ignorant, so I asked him if maybe the recipe called for a slab of bacon. He only responded that Italians will put anything in a cioppino.

When I next saw my Italian friend, I went right over to him with my obvious question, mentioning that even the Swiss chef had not heard of pig nipples. What are they, I asked him, and how do you get them?

He started to laugh. He was afraid I would put the recipe in a drawer and never look at it. He included this outrageously fictitious ingredient to see if I was paying attention. There may be such a thing as pig nipples in real life, but they certainly don't go into a cioppino!

Unusually Crunchy

I've become accustomed to unusual orders and the downright strange eating habits of folks, having worked in the restaurant business for many years. But the man who ordered the escargot appetizer and proceeded to eat the shells as well as the escargot itself dumbfounded me. It was the loud, crunching noise that first got my attention. As I watched, he chewed the shell and neatly deposited the masticated heap onto the plate. One by one, he worked through six shells, and when I say it dumbfounded me, I seriously could not think of anything to say to him...I just watched.

When he had finished, I gingerly cleared his plate from the table. Since escargot was all he had ordered, I brought him his bill. As he was leaving, he casually asked, "Are you going to be getting any cracked crab?"

Favorites and Regulars

Every day I am surrounded by lots of great food as an essential part of my job, with many items that are appealing to me. I wouldn't work in a restaurant if I did not appreciate their particular offerings. Despite the large variety, I tend to fall back to my favorite dishes, still enjoying that cheese omelet as often as I can. Customers seem to be embarrassed about always ordering the same item, but I tell them not to be. It's what we want in a restaurant; to have a customer, or even an employee, enjoy his food so much he can't wait to have it again. We love our regular customers, with their regular orders.

Sometimes customers' usual requests become their identifying characteristics. One waitress referred to her customer as "the black coffee and water with no ice," and I knew who she was talking about. Since I don't always know my customers' names, I remember them as "salmon pasta, hold the asparagus," "New York steak, extra rare," or "Chicken Cordon Bleu, with a side of béarnaise sauce."

For years, I worked all day on Sundays and had my own "regular order." I began my workday in the morning for the brunch shift, then took a break and returned later for dinner. I looked forward to Sundays, not for the long hours and hard work, but for my employee meals. Just before the restaurant opened, and our day began, I asked the chef for a favorite omelet or some of his famous scrambled eggs. I later found out why his eggs were so fluffy and delicious; they were made with heavy cream!

Early afternoon, after the breakfast and brunch crowd had finished, the kitchen changed gears. The set-up for dinner was different, including many sauces simmering on the stove. Any remnant of the breakfast menu was put away except for the bacon because it was served throughout the day: folded into an omelet or layered onto a cheeseburger. Considered an essential topping for the sauteed calves' liver offered at dinnertime, it was kept available in a covered pan. I uncovered that pan of bacon and helped myself repeatedly. I even showed the new waiters and waitresses how to help themselves after their shift. One day the chef told me that I had eaten a half-pound of bacon that day. Each piece was an ounce and I had eaten eight!

Despite my bacon raids, I wasn't through eating for the day. Once the dinner service was over, the entire staff was lucky enough to sit down and have a proper meal before we went home. My usual Sunday evening order was a pepper steak, a slice of New York strip covered with black peppercorns, served with our famous potatoes au gratin.

When times changed and the restaurant stopped serving our very popular Sunday brunch, a lot of folks asked me why. I explained that they could not stay open because I was eating them out of business!

SO MANY CHOICES!

One evening a customer asked me, "How is the Rack of Lamb"? The Rack of Lamb happens to be one of my favorite dishes on the menu, so it was easy for me to launch into a full description of how it's first washed and then brushed with some mustard for tenderizing. The meat is seared in a very hot oven to the desired temperature and doneness before being glazed with a garlic wine sauce. My enthusiasm for the lamb came through, with my customers' mouths watering in anticipation. The lovely rack lived up to their expectations. The customers seemed surprised by my expertise, whereas I believe it ought to be commonplace. When I'm dining in a restaurant, I want a server to be knowledgeable about the food being served. Enthusiasm is an added plus!

I have to admit that I don't like every dish offered on the menu, but my personal preferences should play no part in my customer's decision, and I should be able to describe every offering in the restaurant in detail.

A customer surprised me one day when he said, "I'll have the chicken, if that's all right with you!" I was astonished at his suggestion that it made a difference to me what he ordered. He said that the last time he had asked for the Roasted Chicken with Garlic Mushroom sauce, I had "made a face." I did not remember the encounter. Perhaps it had been a long day and my feet hurt, or something else had flashed across my mind at that moment. I realized then that my presentations are very meaningful to my customers and vowed to be more careful in the future.

FOND MEMORIES

An older woman sat with her family at one of my tables and listened as we were telling restaurant stories. As the group was leaving, she took me aside and said she clearly remembered the first time her parents took her to a restaurant in a fancy hotel in San Francisco in 1940. She was ten years old at the time. She was very happy when the waiter asked her what she would like to have. She knew exactly what she wanted, all her favorites: watermelon, tomato soup and a Coca-Cola.

VEGETABLE DILEMMAS

I've discovered that in my profession, when describing the menu items, you have to be honest. For example, if I've told a customer the dish has no onions, it better not have any onions when I present it. Onions, bell peppers and mushrooms seem to bring out the worst in customers, as if I'm personally making them eat something that they despise. When they're unwanted, these vegetables can apparently "ruin the whole dinner!"

One man did not like carrots. He was emphatic about it. If there were carrots of any sort on his plate, I had to take it back to the chef and have them removed. I learned that the hard way, by being scolded and making a return trip to the kitchen.

One evening, our chef baked cauliflower

and topped it with a cheesy crust as the vegetable offering. He watched as the plates were returned to the kitchen one by one with the cauliflower untouched. He was incensed! "Peas or beans are what I'm making from now on! That's all they'll eat!" I asked him for a plate of the cauliflower for dinner that night. It was delicious, but we never saw it again.

All restaurants should have the servers taste the food. It makes it difficult for the server when the Chef prepares something new and tells us to sell it without knowing what it tastes like. It could look very good, but be laden with a particular spice or flavor that may be all right for one patron, but a turn off for someone else, and of course, it could possibly be made with onions.

Our restaurant menu listed a kid's steak. It was a chopped sirloin steak, which is really a hamburger, served with mushroom gravy. I learned quickly that most of the kids did not want the sauce or the mushrooms. To make matters worse, one evening the side vegetable choice was creamed spinach. One little boy told me that the mushrooms and the spinach made this the worst dinner ever.

I tried to make it better for him by singing him the Popeye song, about how spinach makes you strong to the finish. He tried a small bite, but really did not want to eat it. Since he wasn't eating, he was drawing and coloring on our paper placemats, waiting for dessert. He was looking forward to ice cream, but his father teased him by saying that there was only spinach ice cream. This made the little boy start to cry. I felt sorry for him and quickly brought him vanilla ice cream with chocolate sauce. After that, he presented me with a drawing of Popeye, complete with exaggerated muscles on his arms, holding a can of spinach. He did not like his dinner at all, but the picture he drew for me told me that at least he liked my song.

WHAT'S GOOD TONIGHT?

On occasion, customers will ask me what they should order. I look at them very thoughtfully and ask, "Now what did you eat yesterday? What are you having tomorrow? I'm looking to keep a little variety in your diet."

If that doesn't help them decide, I've been known to ask them to close their eyes and I will describe each item. Sometimes they are so surprised by my approach that I find them staring at me. I explain that closing their eyes is one way to make an assessment of the menu options, which can help in making their selection.

Sometimes this can backfire as it did when one customer indignantly stated, "You're going to tell me what I should have and I'm not going to close my eyes." When that happened, I took a deep breath and realized that this approach isn't for everyone.

I have a regular customer who never chooses his own dinner. He says, "Feed me." I have served him many years, and enjoy picking out what I think is exceptional that evening. He has always enthusiastically enjoyed my choices for him and I believe he's sampled everything on the menu. This is where it can be fun and rewarding for me as the server, by showcasing my expertise and stepping up the hospitality.

If I do a good job of helping customers choose their dinner, everybody's happy. My style of asking people to close their eyes may be unique, but my intention is only to ensure a pleasant experience in our restaurant.

NEW DIET PLAN

A lady customer was watching her calories. She asked me not to bring her regular order of cheesecake piled high with whipped cream. She was going to sacrifice for the sake of her diet. Instead, she asked for just the bowl of whipped cream. We have to cut back where we can!

CHICKEN-FRIED

When my Mother and I were in Kansas, we stopped at a roadside cafe that offered three items: chicken-fried steak, chicken-fried fish or chicken-fried chicken. I don't remember which two we ordered because they both tasted about the same to us. We commented that this was not the way we would eat if we were at home, and to have "chicken-fried" as the only menu options seemed very limiting to us. But, once in a while, it is a very tasty and hearty meal.

Chicken-fried steak, also known as pan-fried steak or country-fried steak, is a very popular and delicious breakfast offering in my restaurant. It is a tenderized beef cube steak, pounded flat, dredged with flour and egg then covered with breadcrumbs and fried. It got its name because it's similar to the preparation of fried chicken.

A large group of young people came in for breakfast one morning and ordered from our varied menu. Pancakes with bacon, oatmeal, granola and yogurt, French toast and omelets were some of the selections. One young man ordered the country-fried steak. I asked him how he wanted his eggs cooked and what kind of toast, as this was all included with his order.

Everyone seemed happy as I was carrying out the plates, placing the correct one in front of each hungry guest who ordered it. When I got to the young man, I put his plate down and said, "Here's your chicken-fried steak." He looked at me and said, "I don't eat chicken."

I shrugged off the comment with "That's OK, because this is the chicken-fried steak that you ordered." I put extra emphasis on the word "steak." Again, he said, "I don't eat chicken."

This time I looked to the rest of the table for support as I explained that "chicken-fried" is the method of preparation, and this is actually a beefsteak. His girlfriend glared at me, and said, "He said he doesn't eat chicken!"

All right, then. I gave up, picked up the plate and calmly asked the customer what I could bring him for breakfast. He ordered a hamburger, a *beef* hamburger, which I urgently called into the kitchen and soon placed in front of him with no explanation.

And that is how I know first hand that our country-fried, or chicken-fried steak is so good. I ate it myself.

A REAL HOLIDAY

One chef told me that he didn't like working in the restaurant through the holidays when other people had the day off. His idea was to have a national holiday where nobody had to work. When asked what he would do on that day, he responded, "I would take my girlfriend out for dinner."

CHAPTER TWO

First Impressions

"A first impression is so important that it can make
or break the entire experience."

An Unwelcome Guest

Walk into a restaurant and look around. Feel the ambience: the lighting, the decor, the serenity or hustle and bustle. Is there an aroma of fine food in the air, and the soft sounds of people conversing and enjoying their meals? Are you greeted warmly by the staff? Does everything seem as it should? A first impression is so important that it can make or break the entire experience. First impressions can become lasting impressions.

A friend and I visited a small local restaurant a few years ago. It was a late hour, and the place was filled with folks who had spent an evening out and were grabbing a bite before going home. As we waited by the door to be seated, I watched the servers moving quickly through the crowd and the cooks who were working in an open kitchen. We stood a few minutes and had a chance to take in the whole atmosphere. In front of us was a lit, glass display case filled with tantalizing desserts.

I checked out the baked goods: layer cakes, homemade pastries and pies set out to entice the customer with the anticipation of a lovely dessert to look forward to. Something caught my attention. There was a bit of movement, something out of the ordinary and I looked a little more closely and saw something I should never see.

I got the attention of my friend discreetly, and he too noticed that there was a visitor among the desserts. In plain sight, a mouse was on a small plate containing a slice of apple pie. He was nibbling from the sharp end of the wedge. It was a cute picture, one that could be immortalized in ceramic. Oh dear, I thought. All the attention to detail that had gone into this restaurant, and that's the first thing we see: a rodent! Cute, but still a rodent.

We never said a word to the

staff. We were seated and ordered some eggs, potatoes and toast. Our server was friendly and asked us if we wanted to have some dessert before we went home, and we just smiled and said, "No, thanks."

THE PEDIGREED WAITRESS

Our restaurant staff was introduced to a new waitress, recently hired. She came armed with a six-page resumé showing her server and managerial experience in several posh San Francisco restaurants. She so impressed the manager that he told us to listen carefully and learn everything we could from her. He felt she was almost pedigreed...came with her papers and everything. The first day I worked with her, it was painfully obvious that she was not now, and never had been, a waitress.

I had to remind her to serve a steak knife with the Rack of Lamb, a minor mistake, I thought at first. But apparently she did not even understand the concept of proper service of courses. She brought every item the customers ordered, but failed to clear any used dishes. Her tables were cluttered and piled high with empty appetizer plates and soup bowls.

As a courtesy, I helped her deliver the main course to one of her tables when I discovered there was literally nowhere to set the plates. The customers were doing the best they could and had started stacking the dishes up. They looked at me plaintively and asked if I could please remove some of these plates. The "exceptionally gifted waitress" appeared embarrassed when I apologized to the table, and essentially took over and finished serving them.

A favorable first impression along with a false resumé got her in the door, but did not help her keep the job.

A Visit to Valhalla

It was Thanksgiving Day in the late seventies and we were looking for a restaurant that served lobster. The places that were open that day, not surprisingly, were serving turkey dinners. We finally phoned Sally Stanford's Valhalla, and were pleased to discover that they had their full menu available, including lobster tail. Sally Stanford and her Sausalito waterfront restaurant had a reputation for a high-class clientele, and we knew that although it might be an expensive holiday dinner, it would be a memorable one.

Sally was famous for having been San Francisco's best-known and classiest Madam. She was later elected Mayor of Sausalito, and opened her restaurant in 1950. Her reputation preceded her; everybody knew of Sally Stanford. We made a reservation, dressed in our finest attire, and arrived at the appointed hour.

As soon as we entered, we saw and heard the famous Sally herself, sitting at the end of the bar. She looked quite diminutive in her signature barber chair. I expected to see someone as large as her reputation, but here was a small, older woman yelling at one of the employees, "You tell them I said so. Who the hell do they think they are?" It was a startling first impression, to walk into an exclusive, fancy restaurant and hear the owner bellowing and swearing.

The interior of the restaurant reminded us of a bordello, intentionally reminiscent of Sally's background. For a pre-dinner cocktail, we were ushered into a waiting room decorated with red velvet couches, overstuffed pillows and textured fabric wallpaper. The restaurant was filled with fur-clad ladies and tuxedoed gentlemen.

We were then escorted into an

empty side room with extra banquet tables stacked up against the walls. I joked that our clothes were not fancy enough for the main dining room, so they put us in the storage room. We didn't care; we were there for the lobster and we still had large picture windows that overlooked San Francisco Bay. The sun was setting over the water and the view was beautiful. I remember the wine we ordered, Wente Brothers Grey Reisling, a popular choice at the time. And our lobster was cooked to perfection.

Soon another group was seated at a table next to ours. A couple with a small child apparently had been exiled to the storage room along with us. We took our time in order to savor our lobster, so the other family finished their dinner before us and left. Our waiter was very friendly, and we asked him if we were correct in recognizing one of our dining companions as Van Morrison, the rock star. Just then the man himself returned to the storage room to retrieve his forgotten scarf. He heard our remark and gave us a smile. We had eaten Thanksgiving dinner with Van Morrison and his family, just the five of us, at Sally Stanford's Valhalla.

Before we left to go home, I went into the Ladies Room. A waitress was in there washing up. I told her that I had just enjoyed a marvelous meal, and that I was glad to be at the famous Valhalla with Sally Stanford. I mentioned that I knew of Sally's biography entitled *Lady of the House* by Bob Patterson and asked the waitress if she had seen the recent film made from the book, starring Dyan Cannon. She told me that Sally did not like the film, and had said that, "Dyan Cannon was no lady." I later read that Sally Stanford actually said, "She did not have what it takes to play me; granted, that's a tall order!"

Sally Stanford died in 1982, leaving behind a legacy of tales from a memorable period in San Francisco history. We had come to Valhalla for the lobster, and also for the experience of seeing the notorious Sally. She certainly lived up to her reputation for being a strong-willed personality, as well as providing a somewhat questionable first impression. It was interesting for us to see a part of the Old San Francisco still around even though we were relegated to viewing it from a storage room.

A Young Man's Recollection

A customer of mine recently told me this story. He grew up in Toledo, Ohio. For a vacation one year, his father took the whole family to Chicago to visit the Research and Science Museum. Afterwards, they were excited to learn that they were going to dinner in a posh restaurant. My friend said that he and his brothers and sisters weren't accustomed to the unusual selections on this fancy restaurant menu, so all of them ordered the spaghetti.

The table next to them ordered the "Duck under Glass." The family watched the fanfare of the duck being carried out on a platter under a big cover to be presented. When the cover was lifted, there was a huge gasp. Apparently the waiter had picked up the wrong platter without checking first and presented his customers with a platter of a carcass of someone's leftovers.

In his embarrassment and hasty retreat back to the kitchen, the waiter collided with another waiter carrying a tray laden with the dinners for my friend's family. There was a big crash, and a bigger mess with spaghetti now mixed up with the leftover carcass all over the floor. The neighboring table left in disgust, with no dinner, presumably never to return.

My friend remembers the museum as being enjoyable. But the huge mistake in the restaurant was the most memorable for the kids, and made a lasting impression.

First Contact

I telephoned a restaurant one evening to inquire about their menu, and asked if they were serving any steaks. Whoever answered the phone gave me a surprising response. She told me that they did have steak on the menu, but the beef was tough and I should order the lamb.

I did not expect to hear such a negative remark. Her comment left me with the impression that the food was not high quality. With only one phone call and a short conversation, I lost interest in dining at that restaurant.

If I worked there, I would never say such a thing on the telephone, even if it were true. I have repeated this story many times when training new employees as an example of what not to say on the phone. It is the job of the server to steer the diner towards a better choice of meat once seated, but first and foremost employees should promote the business and get the customer excited about coming in to dine.

A Personal Touch

I have been on the other end of an initial conversation about the menu, and the tables were turned. I answered the telephone at work one day and was asked about our menu choices. I felt it was part of my job to entice a prospective customer into the restaurant, so I tried to enthusiastically describe some of our popular dishes.

The manager overheard me and later advised me not to take the time to read the menu, and that I should only refer the callers to the restaurant's website, as all the information is available online. I did not agree. Our restaurant's unique personality cannot be truly felt online and the caller might find it dismissive to be told to go somewhere else for the information.

This prospective customer was making the effort to call

us personally, perhaps to have a specific question answered or to get a general feel for our restaurant. The ambience and character of a restaurant is important and can be positively presented through a simple phone conversation. By speaking to potential customers, taking time to share favorite dishes, I am able to offer an invitation to come join us. The details, such as location, hours and pricing can be researched on the web, but nothing takes the place of personal contact, especially in the hospitality business.

WEEKEND IN MONTEREY

Every server deserves a nice weekend traveling, relaxing and dining out. One time on a trip to Monterey, we treated ourselves to a uniquely California experience that did not start at a restaurant, but ended on a memorable note for someone in my business.

One of the most beautiful drives in California is along our Pacific coast on Highway 1. Each turn brings another awe-inspiring vista of blue ocean, surf and rocky cliffs into view. In the late seventies, we drove south along that route to visit Monterey for the weekend. I remember it well because it was Good Friday, Friday the 13th and

a full moon. I thought it would be an auspicious weekend to have a short vacation with some friends.

We went to Esalen, a retreat situated high on the cliffs overlooking the ocean. Some of the wonderful and unique features of the place are the outdoor hot tubs. They are carved from the cliffs and fed by a natural hot spring. At that time, the tubs were open to the public at night. We paid a fee and entered around 11 PM with the intention of spending the night soaking in the warm water, listening to the waves crash along the surf line beneath us. The light from the full moon danced over the water. It was beautiful and surreal. The sea air was cool, cold actually, so we hunkered down with our shoulders under the water.

As you might imagine, we didn't want to move when our time was up, at 6 AM. Some workers quietly came through and mentioned that we had only a few more minutes, but nobody was ready to end such a magical experience.

I guess the folks at Esalen are used to that and know how to handle it. At the appointed hour, they came through and pulled up the plugs for all the tubs. The warm water quickly drained out. Shivering, wet and dressing quickly, we were soon in our car with the heater on and realized that we were hungry.

The morning sun was golden and it was going to be a very pretty day. We were happy and soothed from our night in the tubs. I saw a sign for a restaurant, open for breakfast that read "Trout and Eggs," so we pulled in.

We stood for a while in the doorway of the small cafe. We were not greeted or even acknowledged. In fact, it felt as if we were given the brush off by the obviously local crowd. This gave us a chance to look around and check out the ambience, or lack thereof. First impressions, again, can make or break the whole experience. We finally took a seat and still waited. Other diners were eating and watching us.

I noticed that our table was not clean. I then looked at the candleholder on the table and it had about an inch of dust on it. Then the dog came in.

This was a Saint Bernard, a large one, I'm guessing about a hundred pound animal. Our family had a beloved Saint Bernard dog named Tina, and I know the breed. The dog stopped just inside the door, sat down and used her back leg to scratch herself. In the horizontal light of the morning, I could see gobs of dog hair flying through the air. We still had not been offered a menu. I turned to my friends and said, "We're leaving." They protested that it was my idea that we stop here, but I insisted and we left.

What a contrast: from the warm welcome and companionship at the hot tubs, to the cold and dirty restaurant. We were back to reality. We did find another diner along the road and had a mediocre breakfast. It has been many years since we spent the weekend in Monterey but I remember it well.

WORLD CLASS SERVICE?

A friend told me about a trip to Southern California a few years ago. He went there to attend a symposium held on the magnificent Queen Mary. The ship has become a famous tourist destination in Long Beach, but was built for first class transatlantic travel, in the days when ocean liners were the way to go. Her maiden voyage was in 1936. She plied the Atlantic waters until she served as a troop carrier in World War II and was retired from service in 1967, when she was bought by the City of Long Beach. Although stationary, she has been through some "rough waters" since, operating under many different managing companies including the Disney Corporation. Today she sits proudly at Pier J, with several restaurants, a 300-room hotel, a maritime museum and convention space.

The symposium was a meeting of World War II fighter

aces from both sides, with many famous pilots. Hub Zemke, a USAAF ace; Adolf Galland, General of the Luftwaffe; and Gunther Rall, renowned fighter ace and head of the West German Luftwaffe, were among the keynote speakers. It was hosted by Virginia Bader, niece of Douglas Bader, the famous English pilot who commanded a squadron for the RAF after losing both legs in an accident in 1930.

There is a camaraderie and shared honor among the pilots who were one-time enemies. The symposium was well attended and included a banquet that my friend dubbed the worst hundred-dollar dinner he ever had. What a shame, to have so many distinguished men in attendance, and to be served such an awful meal. In fact, Hub Zemke was kept so busy talking with the attendees, he did not have a chance to eat, and everybody thought that he was lucky.

For the banquet, which was supposed to be the highlight of the event, round tables were set for eight and the chairs were quite close together, which made for uncomfortably crowded dining. Soup, served as the first course, apparently tasted like "seafood salt." The table discussion continued about the sorbet, served after the soup to cleanse the palate. The flavor was indiscernible, almost tasteless: was it lemon or orange? No one seemed to know, and the question remained unanswered. The main dish was of poor quality, and not even memorable.

The final nail in the coffin was the service. My friend asked for a refill for his water. The waiter brought a pitcher of ice water, picked up the drinking glass and started to pour. When it was apparent that he was overpouring and there was going to be some spillage, the waiter shocked

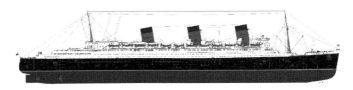

everyone when he quickly put the water pitcher under the full glass that my friend had been drinking from and let the overflow run back into the pitcher. Oh no! Letting dirty water run back into the serving vessel! That should never, ever happen. I'm still disgusted whenever I retell the story and I wasn't even there. My friend did not drink any more water and actually stopped eating his dinner.

Today, the stately Queen's reputation has been restored and I've heard the restaurants aboard are award-winning. Apparently when my friend visited, the management company at that time did not understand the importance of quality, of showing respect for their guests nor did they comprehend the significance of their venue.

Once a visitor has a bad experience, it is quite difficult to forget. In the hospitality business, we must be mindful that it is almost impossible to overcome a customer's reluctance to return after having an unpleasant first impression.

CHAPTER THREE

Behind the Scenes

"The kitchen is either very quiet or very busy,
seldom a happy medium."

A Comedy of Errors

I was once asked to work a Breakfast Club to serve sixty people while they listened to a speaker. The club was just starting up and was to be a weekly event. It sounded fun to do, possibly informative, and I was going to make a bit of extra cash. Starting at 6 AM, I thought the early hour was going to be the main challenge. Boy, was I wrong!

When I arrived at 5 AM, there was no cook. It turns out I was responsible for cooking the food, serving the breakfast and then cleaning up afterwards. As Thor will tell you, I am no cook. I can prepare a meal for the two of us, and can bake a delicious cake, but professionally preparing breakfast for sixty people is a real challenge for a novice.

The first obstacle was the stove. It was an old, dirty gas stove that needed the pilot light lit. That took me about fifteen minutes. I tried not to panic. I can do this, I kept telling myself, as I crawled behind the stove looking for the gas outlet. I had worn nice clothes to serve in, and my blouse was already dirty. Oh, well...

Sausages and bacon just needed to be put on baking sheets and warmed, so no problem there. But wait, the sheet pans did not fit into the oven—a small setback. I searched in the kitchen and found serving trays, which at home I would never put in the oven, and covered them with frozen bacon and sausages. The oven was just warming, and, oh yeah, the breakfast folks might want some coffee. There was no automatic coffee machine. There were only two old percolators. Thanks to my Mom, I knew how to make coffee in the percolators, but you can't rush these old machines. When the early guests started arriving, there was a wait for the coffee, which is not good. Don't panic; just keep going, I said to myself.

The good news was that there were sweet rolls and bagels ready to go, and I arranged them on platters along side some pitchers of orange juice. The tables had been set up the night before, thank God, because there was no way I could have done all that by myself. I told the guests to have some juice and that the coffee should be ready soon. The percolators had just started.

There was supposed to be scrambled eggs served. I can obviously break a few eggs, but I had no idea how many to cook for sixty people. I decided I could figure it out, so I found a frying pan and began looking for eggs. No eggs. But in the freezer there were plastic bags of liquid, scrambled eggs that looked like survival food to be consumed only in an emergency. I mentioned that they were frozen, right? There were no instructions on the hard plastic bags of yellow stuff, other than to place in water and be careful not to boil. I searched for a pot large enough to fill with water and got the fire going under the huge pot of maybe three or four gallons of water. I stuffed three bags of the frozen eggs in the lukewarm water. As I later found out, that was enough eggs for a hundred and eighty servings.

Some of the guests started to come into the kitchen looking for coffee. I didn't blame them. The percolators were working fine, only another five minutes to go, but any delay in coffee service is unacceptable for a breakfast club. Keep your cool, Linda. Maybe the meat is ready. Burned! Most of the sausages and bacon were black and extra crispy. I separated out the edible ones and put them on dinner plates since the serving platters were now hot from the oven and caked with burned grease. The kitchen did not have a nice warm smell to it, but at least the coffee was ready. I filled up a few carafes and started another batch. What's another fifteen minutes? The carafes were soon emptied and there was a clamor for more coffee.

Now I had a lot of company in the kitchen with me. Apparently what was going on in the kitchen was much more interesting than the speaker they hired for the breakfast meeting.

The eggs were still frozen and someone noticed the plastic bags of yellow stuff in the pot, and went out yelling to everyone else that we were serving plastic eggs and not to eat them. I agreed with him. At this point, I was just trying to be cool and not show any distress. What a pro!

The breakfast was a disaster. The kitchen was a mess. The folks only had some orange juice, bagels, coffee and burnt bacon. They were very nice to me and seemed to understand my dilemma. They left with a good story to tell. I was left with the cleanup. Not only did I have to clear the dining room and reset all the tables back to their original places, I also had to clean up the whole kitchen.

Sixty pounds of eggs went into the garbage with most of the sausages and bacon. The dishwasher was ancient, spewing sudsy water all over the floor, but at least it washed all the plates. The oven platters and pots had to be scrubbed by hand and the percolators needed to be emptied and broken down. I called Thor for back up. He arrived and the two of us were there until almost 4 PM. We left the place sparkling clean, even mopping the floor, leaving everything better than its original condition.

I went home exhausted. I got a call from my employer who told me that he was a little disappointed with the way things had turned out and that he would dock my pay for the wasted food, especially the eggs. He told me that the breakfast club would be meeting the next week and that I should have a more organized method by then. He seemed a little surprised when I declined the offer.

I didn't even care about the money at that point, and he actually took a few weeks to pay me what amounted to about fifty bucks, after all the deductions. He did comment on how nice I had left the kitchen, and asked if he could call me in the future for other assignments. I usually don't like to burn any bridges, but I decided this one is permanently closed.

QUIETLY EFFICIENT SERVICE

The best service in a restaurant is when the service is hardly noticed. Why do I say that? Theoretically, the emphasis in a restaurant should be a good meal and conviviality, in other words, the gathering of friends. What is going on behind the scenes should never be the focal point.

A successful experience is when the food tastes good, everything goes well and the customers have a nice time. This happens only when all the employees quietly and unobtrusively do their job. My previous story about the customers all coming into the kitchen to see what was wrong, was truly "a kitchen nightmare."

For restaurant employees, keeping up the pace while maintaining tranquility can sometimes be challenging, as every table in the restaurant is unique, with their own priorities and time schedule.

However, there is a big difference between quiet and unobtrusive service and neglecting the duties of a server. How many times have you been in a restaurant where the employees are unavailable or inattentive? Perhaps they are all standing around at the coffee machine only interested in having a conversation about their weekend plans, or, worse yet, discussing personal or personnel problems in the dining room.

Customers see and hear what is being done, what is not being done and what is being said. When kitchen problems or servers' antics become the focal point of the experience, it rapidly destroys the image the restaurant is trying to present.

Besides the obvious part of my job which is serving food, I have an obligation to ensure my guests' comfort. I accomplish this by pretending that I am the customer. I put myself in their place and ask, what do I need and what am I seeing and hearing? A customer who is sitting in a restaurant cannot get up and get a spoon for his coffee, or an extra napkin. That's my job, to notice the little details.

If the server is paying attention, the work can be accomplished efficiently and without fanfare, which is why I say the service should be so smooth that it's almost invisible.

Behind The Scenes At The Palace

All the employees at the large hotels in San Francisco are members of a union. You can't be hired if you're not a union member and you can't get a union card if you don't have a job. My first lesson in union politics back in the seventies was that it came down to who you knew. I knew my landlady's best friend. She was a waitress at the Palace Hotel and was leaving her job. She walked me into the hotel, introduced me to the manager, and then escorted me down to the union hiring hall. Soon I was a certified union member with a job.

The Minute Chef coffee shop at the corner of Market Street and New Montgomery was my domain for the next three years. There were no tables, only a U-shaped counter surrounded by stools. It was set quite high so the patrons had to step up to be seated. We worked inside the counter with no way out other than through the kitchen. My co-worker Ruth was a life-long waitress and had been at the hotel for many years. She taught me the ropes and introduced me to the regular characters of our little corner of the city. I soon knew all the deliverymen, and made friends with the baker who brought the donuts every morning.

I was fortunate to work with the best short order cook

in the business, Ray. He told me once that the most time-consuming item to prepare on the breakfast menu was the toast. So he "dropped" the toast the first thing. He was fast! Fluffy scrambled eggs and perfect pancakes and French toast flew out of his little window, piping hot for us to serve.

On the other side of Ray's breakfast station was another kitchen serving the Tudor Room dining room and bar. I was introduced to the cooks and the servers, who started their shifts at 10:30 AM to prepare for the 11:30 lunch opening. I met the Maitre d'Hotel named Walter White and all the professional old-time waiters of San Francisco. Walter was an imposing man, always in a tuxedo with a black eye patch over one eye. He and I became friends as I made a hot chocolate for him almost every day.

At the Minute Chef, we served most of the hotel guests and VIPs including the General Manager's wife. She arrived every morning accompanied by her little dog. Her usual order for breakfast was an English muffin, one egg and a half grapefruit, which I sectioned with a special knife. She was an elegant Hungarian in expensive clothes, and reminded me of Zsa Zsa Gabor. Walter told me a bit about her. When she dined in his dining room, she did not like to sit on her skirts. She thought they would then be wrinkled. So before she sat down, she always pulled her skirt up over the back of her dining chair! He liked to stand behind her to help her with her chair, hoping to glimpse what he could.

My breakfast co-worker and I kept very busy, but had enough time to get to know each other. Ruth will probably always remember me because of the new drink I introduced to her. The hotel pantry was completely stocked with anything that might be requested by the guests. In those days, the policy was lenient and we servers helped ourselves to pretty much anything we wanted, within reason. I love buttermilk and drink it often. It is even better mixed with a little fruit juice, especially prune. The resulting concoction tastes like kefir, a yogurt-type drink. I found it filling, nutritious and delicious. I offered some to Ruth one day as she was leaving to go home. Apparently it had a strong laxative effect on her. She told me the next day that when she pulled into her driveway, she didn't think she had enough time to get her keys out and open her front door. She ran into her neighbor's house to use the bathroom. Her experience probably wasn't as funny as it seemed to me. Prune juice and buttermilk, still a favorite of mine!

Ruth drove a vintage Ford Thunderbird convertible, aqua blue. She parked it behind the Palace Hotel in the alley and never locked it. She found homeless men sleeping in her car so often that it became commonplace for her. I asked her why she didn't lock her car. She told me that if they wanted to get in they would, and she didn't want the fabric roof of the convertible slashed. She took a large stick out to the car with her after her shift, brandished it and the sleeper would get out without incident.

Ruth, Ray and Walter were the core team working behind the scenes to make the hotel run smoothly with quiet efficiency. I learned a lot in the small kitchen of the Palace Hotel. I was a part of the pulse of the City for a period of time, working fast-paced early morning breakfast shifts with a team of professionals. Each had their own stories, interests and strengths, and helped me become a professional waitress.

There were other employees who came and went, not staying very long for various reasons. A cook named Crazy Richard, overwhelmed by a very busy lunch shift one day, lay down behind the stove, refusing to get up and was fired on the spot. A room-service waiter put on an apron and finished putting out everyone's order.

Another cook in the hotel also had to be let go. He was a large man from Brazil, who fixed very strong coffee for us one morning, saying it was how they drank it in Brazil. I had the shakes for a couple of days. He was very homophobic, making no secret of his dislike for the gay waiters working in the dining room. Their disagreements came to a head one day, with the angry Brazilian cook chasing a waiter through the dining room with a knife. We all figured he had drunk some of his own coffee.

PRESSURES IN THE KITCHEN

"If you can't stand the heat, get out of the kitchen…
but put the knives down first."

Kitchen pressures are legendary. When orders are coming in fast and furiously, hot working conditions along with short tempers can sometimes be a recipe for disaster. One head chef told me that banter in the kitchen can relieve some of the pressure of the job. He doesn't discourage the practice, but insists that it should be in good taste, and never leave the kitchen.

The pressure can sometimes bring out quirks in our personalities. Each employee has their own way of handling tense situations. Yelling and screaming are common reactions to the chaos of a busy kitchen. I'm known for telling a joke, or doing a silly dance to bring laughter into the situation.

The kitchen is either very quiet or very busy, seldom a happy medium. One pantry worker, in charge of the appetizers, salads and desserts made the comment, "All at once or nothing!" He was right because customers naturally want to eat their breakfast, lunch and dinner at the appropriate hour. When customers come in all together, filling up the breakfast counter or dining room, the energy picks up. The kitchen suddenly transforms to high activity. Pots and pans are brought out and slammed down, sizzling sounds come from the grill and fryer, cooks are yelling instructions, servers are calling out orders, plates are clanking...as one waitress often declared loudly, "It's show time!"

PILFERING ON A GRAND SCALE

A waiter at The Fairmont Hotel told me a story he heard many years ago about Maggie, a long-time waitress. She had been at the landmark hotel in San Francisco so long that she watched the owner's children and grandchildren grow up, feeding them breakfast each morning before they went off to school. Obviously she was on friendly terms with the owners, the Swig family.

One day, the family was discussing replacing all the china in the hotel. The Fairmont was famous for lovely chinaware, embossed with the hotel's logo in gold leaf. Maggie told them not to make any changes. She explained that most of the regular guests already had a complete set in their homes, and any upgrades would mean the collecting would have to start all over again.

On that same note, Mike, the owner of a small, local hamburger joint thought he might as well benefit from any pilfering. He had the soda glasses printed with the inscription, "Stolen from Mike's at the Crossroads."

WHERE'S THE CHICKEN?

After the hustle and bustle of a busy shift, it's good to sit down to have a little something to eat and drink. It helps us unwind before going home. One evening we were given a special treat as the employees' meal. There were five plates of delicious chicken, potatoes and vegetables on the warming shelf in the kitchen. Fresh, steaming and looking so good, we all anticipated a nice meal. The plates were picked up one by one by the servers and everyone went to our special table to eat, relax, chat and count our tips.

As I stood ready to retrieve my dinner, there were only two plates left. One of my co-workers was taking hers when suddenly she sneezed. This was not a small ladylike sneeze, but a big truck driver sneeze. And not one, but two hard sneezes, all over our plates of food. She did not attempt to turn her head, or cover her mouth. I was horrified. Unfazed, she picked up her germ-laden dinner and carried it into the dining room. I stood frozen, shocked that I had just seen such a disgusting thing.

The chef and the dishwasher both witnessed what had happened. I paused for a moment and realized I really wanted that chicken. I wasn't going to let the other waitress ruin my dinner. I asked the chef if he still had the deep fryer on, and he said he did. I asked him if he would put my two pieces of chicken into the deep fryer for a few minutes. The heat would kill the germs. I prepared myself a new plate and threw the ruined potatoes and vegetables away.

A few minutes later, I joined the staff at the employees' table with the most beautiful golden brown fried chicken on my plate. There were lots of stares and everyone wanted to know how I got such a treat. I said nothing and ate happily, remaining quiet about the circumstances.

Months later, when that co-worker no longer worked with us, I recounted the story to some of my friends. Everyone was horrified. They had a hard time forgetting the image and we talked about it often. It started a running joke in the kitchen after that. Whenever anybody sneezed, we all looked at each other and asked, "Where's the chicken?"

Trainee Shenanigans

I was training a new waiter one day. During the tour of the kitchen, I showed him the large walk-in refrigerator where all the desserts were kept. I had my back to him, and assumed he was listening as I pointed out the whereabouts of the different dessert offerings, like the chocolate mousse and the tiramisu.

As I was about to point out the cheesecake, I stopped in my tracks. In one swift movement, the new employee had grabbed a small plate from the shelf. In under a second, he had un-  wrapped a portion of cheesecake and stuffed the entire thing into his mouth. No wonder he had been quiet. His mouth was so full that he was choking a bit, but I was not going to help him in any way.

I was so surprised by his lack of professionalism. We were not there to eat anything and he had not asked permission. What a way to start a new job! I only said, "They count those!" He continued to make mistakes, and I was secretly relieved that he did not keep the job for very long.

Proper Placements

During a server meeting, our manager was explaining the correct way to prepare the restaurant table for guests. She was carefully demonstrating how to polish the silverware while advising us to make sure the plates, glasses and utensils were straight and evenly spaced. She made an insightful and unforgettable comment. "These are supposed to be place settings, not place throwings."

CHAPTER FOUR

THE FINE ART OF SERVING

"Timing is everything in table service; thinking ahead and using proper time management makes the service efficient and enjoyable."

Too Much Attention

I heard a story recently about two waiters vying for attention from one particular table occupied by an attractive gay couple. When one waiter realized his competitor had forgotten to offer freshly ground pepper for the couples' salads, he rushed over to the table carrying an obscenely large pepper grinder and proceeded to profusely pepper what was left of the customer's salad: one piece of lettuce.

The Art of Pepper Grinding

The obscenely large pepper grinder in the last reminiscence brings to mind a caveat I read somewhere: the quality of a restaurant is often indirectly proportionate to the size of its pepper grinders.

We can add to that caution the new, fancy electronic machines sometimes brought to the table in a posh place to whirr and grind precisely. I once worked at a restaurant known for gimmicks as well as good food, and pepper grinders were considered art. We started out with very long grinders that brought comments from the customers, asking if we needed help in carrying or holding them.

One day some new fancy electronic pepper grinders arrived. They were sleek-looking, rechargeable and easy to fill by turning the base to reveal a large opening. They came in black and white, one for grinding your own salt at the table and one for pepper. As the restaurant owner had planned, they were a conversation piece and I had fun demonstrating them.

As I stood over a table the next evening, holding this new contraption in my hands, I got everyone's attention and asked if anyone would like freshly ground pepper on their salads? One lady grabbed the pepper grinder, and said, "Let me do it! Nobody ever lets me grind the pepper!" She then aggressively turned the base, opening the reservoir of whole peppercorns that poured out, actually gushing over everyone's salads. I quietly picked up all the plates to get completely new salads for everyone. I didn't have to say anything. The pepper lady's friends were all over her, explaining precisely why she's not allowed to handle the pepper grinders.

Moving Up to the Tudor Room

After working at the Minute Chef in the Palace Hotel for a few years, I was offered an opportunity to serve lunch and dinner in The Tudor Room, where I was introduced to fine dining table service. I was familiar with some of the menu because of my time serving in the breakfast place next door but there were also new menu items, each with a specific method of serving. I had to learn how to properly open and serve a bottle of wine, prepare Caesar salads and bone a Rex Sole at the table.

The fish was the hardest for me. Rex Sole can be easily boned, in theory, by starting at the tail, slicing very thinly underneath the bone to carefully lift it out in one piece. The boneless filet is then layered back on top and set before the customer. Sometimes it went so smoothly, even I was impressed. Other times the fish was almost mutilated. I could usually see when I took the fish from the kitchen if it had a good starting point or not. On occasion, I confess that I did it in the kitchen and carefully put it back together so the customer did not see the trouble I was having.

Steak and lobster was the high end offering on the dinner menu. Our table service included removing the lobster from its shell. I became very adept at extracting every last bit of meat, being mindful of its expense. One evening as I was waiting for my two orders of Surf and Turf to emerge from the kitchen, I heard a commotion. Apparently the chef thought the lobsters were overcooked and was refusing to serve them. I was told to tell my guests that there was a slight delay, but the end product would be worth the wait. This situation is hard to believe now in our days of economic stringency, but the chef was going to throw away the two slightly overcooked lobsters and prepare two more. He explained to us that for the money they were paying, they should have excellent quality. I grabbed a styrofoam To Go box and quickly slid it under the two lobsters heading for the trash. I made a slightly risque phone call home, telling my sweetie to melt some butter. Before any wrong conclusions could be drawn, I added, "I'm bringing home lobster!"

Fortunately for me, I never had to learn how to flambé. Just prior to my being hired in the dining room, there was an accident in one of the other San Francisco hotels, and an inexperienced waiter was burned. After that, many restaurants stopped serving anything flambé. It's just as well; it's probably not a good idea for me to be handling an open bottle of alcohol near a flame.

CLOTHES DON'T MAKE THE WOMAN!

In order to work in The Garden Court and The Pied Piper Room at the Palace, I needed the proper uniform. The hotel wanted to maintain an old-style image, so they sent us to Gunne Sax, an upscale dress shop known for Victorian-style, fitted gowns designed by Jessica Mc-Clintock. We were given two expensive long gowns, ruffled with different floral patterns. We looked lovely and charming. So much so that it was a shock when one of the elegantly dressed waitresses, unhappy about her modest tip, ran through the hotel lobby yelling at two older women customers who didn't understand what the fuss was about. The well-dressed but unruly waitress was fired that day.

A TAD MORE

A Chinese busboy once informed me that a particular table had ordered a "funny kind of coffee." When I approached the table, I asked what it was that I could get for them. They responded that they had only asked the young man for a tad more coffee!

HOLIDAY AT THE PALACE

Now that I was a bona fide dining room waitress, I was offered some holiday shifts in the famous Garden Court, wearing my pretty uniform. The Court was known for delicious salads, made with chicken, shrimp or crab with the world-famous Green Goddess dressing. This lovely seven-story, glass-roofed enclosure was the original entrance to the Hotel. The interior floors were rimmed with flowered balconies, so that coming into the newly built Palace in 1875 was an impressive sight. Many old photos depict the Grand Court's circular drive filled with horses and expensive carriages, conveying guests to and fro.

One Christmas, I was scheduled to work helping to serve the fancy buffet. At first, I wasn't happy about working on this holiday, but the elegance of the families coming in to a beautifully decorated room full of history made it worthwhile. The buffet was extensive; it was amazing how much food was available. Eggs Benedict and omelets were offered as well as smoked salmon and kippers with capers, onions and sour cream, and a bowl of caviar served with crackers. Bacon and sausages were in their warming pans, and many homemade sweet rolls, brioche and breads filled festive baskets.

Salad selections and cold items including freshly steamed crabs covered another table. A chef was on hand, dressed in a clean white uniform complete with a toque, to carve roast beef, ham or turkey. The desserts were sinful: pies, eclairs, cream puffs, black forest cake and cheesecake to name a few.

The customers were formally attired, many in velvet dresses trimmed with lace. The young ones were especially cute; boys in suits and girls wearing patent leather shoes and holiday dresses.

It was a memorable festive experience, an excellent day for tips and I brought home a bountiful doggie bag.

TIME MANAGEMENT

A customer of mine who was extra thirsty needed his water glass filled repeatedly. I finally put the pitcher down on his table and left it there. He smiled and said it was nice of me to leave it for him and he was thankful for the extra service.

I found his comment interesting because by leaving the water pitcher, I was doing less work and giving the customer the responsibility of filling his own water glass. Although this particular customer was happy, I made a light-hearted comment about saving myself some time and being a lazy waitress.

As I walked past another table, I asked a customer if he wanted more sauce for his steak. He answered, "When you have the time." I responded that a good waitress takes that into consideration and will only ask to bring something if it's readily available and she has the time.

When a customer asked for more hot water for her tea, saying that it wasn't an immediate need, just sometime whenever I passed by her table. I told her I had better get it right away or time would pass and I'd forget.

Timing is everything in table service, thinking ahead and using proper time management makes the service efficient and enjoyable.

HURRY UP!

One waitress friend of mine is full of energy. She does everything at a fast pace, almost running while at work. I'll never forget the time she was hurrying up some stairs carrying a plate of fried scallops. They were served with french fries, fresh peas and a small paper cup filled with tartar sauce. She tripped and the scallops flew all over, some landing on tables, some on the floor. The french fries and peas were also scattered far and wide.

She quickly recovered and started cleaning up the mess, but couldn't find the cup of tartar sauce. As she came towards me, I could see the small paper cup of sauce was stuck to her forehead. After much merriment, the plate was refilled in the kitchen and my friend wiped off her "dressing", then slowly and carefully served her customer.

My friend recently told me what she remembered

most about the incident was watching the little peas rolling away in different directions and later finding tartar sauce in her hair.

Too Little, Then Too Much

A friend of mine often dined with her family in a local bistro within walking distance from their house. One particular evening, there was a new waitress who did not clear the appetizer and dinner plates as they were emptied. When my friend asked her to please take the dirty dishes, the waitress responded that she only cleared them after they had paid and left! My friend is a very soft-spoken woman, so she gently insisted. Unfortunately the waitress overreacted and retaliated, taking ALL the plates, even one obviously unfinished dinner. My friend said, "We had to stiff her," meaning they left the waitress no tip, and I agreed with her. Rude behavior should never be rewarded.

They really enjoyed having a good restaurant close to their home, so they hesitantly went back to the bistro a few weeks later and thankfully had a different waiter. This dinner was to be a quiet celebration for her husband. The waiter started out a little too attentive to my friend, and it got progressively more obvious as the dinner went on that the waiter was inappropriately flirting; one might say he was hitting on her. Her husband couldn't believe it and exclaimed, "Is this really happening?"

In her calm manner, she finished relating the story to me by saying, "We don't go there anymore."

A Challenging Situation

Restaurant customers come in all shapes and sizes, encompassing all that humanity has to offer. I've told stories of rude people, charming people and everyone in between.

One of my most memorable customers was very different from an average restaurant diner. She happened to have no arms.

This wasn't noticeable right away, as I only saw four people at one of my tables, waiting for me to serve them. I placed glasses of water in front of each guest as I introduced myself and made my initial greeting, listing the specials of the evening. This particular woman used her right foot very adeptly, picking up the glass of water and drinking easily, not spilling a drop. I continued on, casually taking the orders for a cocktail to start their evening.

When I went back to the kitchen, I informed the busboy who was about to deliver bread and butter, that the lady on table #3 had no arms. I told him not to be shocked, and to treat her as he would any other customer.

There was nothing out of the ordinary, no drama at the table. The lady was with her husband and another couple. Everyone seemed to enjoy the evening. The only exception I made was to ask her if she needed a straw or other utensil to help her. She smiled, thanked me for my concern and told me that she was fine. I was impressed with her easygoing nature, and marveled at her ability to live her life to the fullest, despite her disability.

YOUR CHANGE, SIR?

One of my customers has a pet peeve regarding servers, and is quite vocal about it. He used to dine at a cafe owned by a friend of his. The waitress there was a young gal who had a bad habit of asking her customers if they wanted their change when she picked up a cash payment with the check. As my customer explained, he always responded, "Of course, I want my change!"

After this happened a few times, my friend was so annoyed that he broached the subject with the owner. The owner did not see a problem with the waitress asking the question, so did not confront her about it. As a result, my customer no longer frequents that cafe.

He hesitantly brought up the subject with me and wanted my professional opinion. I agreed with him that this is a very bad policy. The server has a responsibility to return the correct change to the customer, period. There should be no presumption of a tip, which is what she was really asking.

There are correct ways to pick up the money for the check. You should always say, "Thank you" and always bring back any change required. Even if it's less than fifty cents, it's the customer's change. Counting out the change to the customer is also very good. If there is an issue, it can be addressed right then and there. This prevents any miscount along the way, as sometimes happens, and both parties can be happy with the transaction.

If there is going to be a tip, that is another matter. Let the customer pay his bill first, which is sometimes considerable these days. A tip is always voluntary, and should never be assumed.

THE RIGHT TIP?

I recently heard about the ultimate response to service that apparently was the worst my friend had ever encountered. I never did hear any of the details, but whatever happened infuriated him so much that he left a tip of eleven pennies, arranged in the shape of a question mark!

CHAPTER FIVE

DINING ROOM DRAMA

"Never speak to me like that. I don't want anyone to think I'm a regular here."

SEVENTIES SHUFFLE

Picture a crowded San Francisco restaurant catering to a gay clientele in the late '70s. This particular restaurant had a garden theme with potted plants, ferns and rattan furniture. It was popular and a friend of mine worked there as a waiter, flitting about under the trellises. Why is it important to indicate that the waiter and clientele were gay? Because then I've instilled a certain degree of drama and flamboyance...something my friend could always provide.

One particularly busy evening the tables were full. A young couple celebrating an anniversary ended up seated at a small table so close to the kitchen that it would occasionally get bumped by the door swinging open, with servers rushing by yelling orders as they passed. The couple seemed distressed and unhappy. My friend passed them a few times and felt sorry for them. On one pass, he "accidentally" tripped over his shoes as he came through, which pushed the door against their little table once more. He kicked up his then-trendy boots and loudly proclaimed, "Damn these heels!" which made the couple chuckle. They then felt included in the commotion and ended up having a fun and memorable anniversary dinner thanks to my dramatic friend.

CRUMBY CUSTOMERS

A wealthy woman used to frequent our restaurant. After numerous visits, I greeted her familiarly and asked if she would like the particular beverage she had previously ordered. I thought that she would be impressed that I remembered, but she shocked me by responding, "Never speak to me like that. I don't want anyone to think I'm a regular here." After that, I just waited on her without comment, day after day, at the same table.

Then another rude situation arose with this customer. She arrived in a new Mercedes one day and was eating lunch when she asked me if I had any bread left over in the kitchen. The old stale bread, brought back from the tables was good enough to feed the birds and I was used to customers asking for it. This request felt different as she was drilling me with her eyes, asking again, "Do you have any bread left over? I'm having guests tonight!"

Maybe our bread is exceptionally good. Another couple arrived one evening, dressed to the nines. The boss greeted them excitedly and showed them to a nice table. He came to me and announced that these were extremely classy customers and to give them VIP treatment. Although they were dressed up, I didn't see what the fuss was about, and I was proven correct. The VIP customers ordered one coffee and one cup of soup that they shared and then asked for the remainder of the bread to take home. At least they only asked for their bread!

TRUCK STOP GENIALITY

A woman recently told me that she and her husband used to do long-haul trucking across the country. She had a lot of experiences with restaurants, roadside diners and truck stops. A busy restaurant with a lot of trucks parked outside indicates a good place to eat, because the truckers 'get around' and tell each other which places to frequent. They're protective of their spots and are usually good customers.

My truck-driving friend told me about an event she recalled from many years before. She and her husband were at a truck stop on the interstate one morning. It was very busy with drivers drinking coffee, talking and filling out their logbooks.

A rude man came in and started yelling loudly for the waitress. He was almost abusive in his tone. The waitress waited on him as best she could, but his attitude never changed and the whole place was aware of the uncomfortable position she was in. When he left, the other patrons noticed that the rude man did not leave any tip for the waitress. My friend talked to her, and mentioned that with all that noise and ruckus, it wasn't fair that there was not even a small tip. The waitress just smiled and shrugged it off with the comment, "That can happen."

Upon hearing that, most of the other customers put their hands in their pockets and drew out a few extra dollars to leave as compensation for the missing tip. It made the waitress' day to be appreciated in such a thoughtful way.

THE BLT JOKE

A customer in a coffee shop ordered a BLT, NT. When the cook asked what the extra NT was, the customer told him it was a BLT, Not Toasted. When the cook asked the customer if he was enjoying his sandwich, the customer answered, "S-H-I-T." The cook was incensed and yelled, "Don't swear at me!" The customer said that he didn't mean to swear, he was just shortening the phrase, "Should've Had It Toasted."

At lunch one day, a customer asked me for a BLT. I asked him the usual questions, what kind of bread he liked and the obligatory, "Do you want fries with that?" Then I asked him if he wanted his bread toasted and he said no. While we were waiting for his order, I told him the BLT joke. He laughed. As I was setting down his lunch, I teased him and said, "I hope it's not S-H-I-T" and he responded that it was F-I-N-E.

INFLUENCING THE WORLD CUP

I was working in a sports bar and the World Cup soccer matches were on, with England playing. The place was crowded and noisy with fans yelling out, rooting for their team. One customer ordered his breakfast and asked for his English muffin to be extra toasted and very dark. I typed in the instruction to the chefs on the computer, "Burn the English," and, what do you know, they lost the game.

NO BABYSITTING

It was Valentine's Day and the restaurant was busy, filled to capacity with tables of two. Red candles on the tables gave a romantic lighting to the room. The place was crowded and some folks were waiting for their tables. All of the servers were carefully serving the couples and keeping the atmosphere quiet and comfortable to maintain the romantic ambience.

As I was walking into the dining room, I was surprised to see a young boy, maybe five or six years old, roaming around. He was small and it would have been easy for us to collide, so I looked for his parents to see if they could keep the youngster at the table and out of the way of the service. I asked the boy where his parents were, and he pointed to a couple sitting at a table for two, enjoying their meal, with no apparent place for the boy to sit. I approached them and excused myself for interrupting, then asked if this was their son. They said yes, but explained that they were there for a romantic dinner. They could not find a babysitter, so they brought him along to run around and entertain himself while they enjoyed their "date."

I felt sorry for the boy, being left alone like that with nothing to do except get in the way. Just then, I looked over and saw him at the top of a small staircase, acting as if he had been shot, and tumbling down the stairs gripping his heart. I hurried over to him to assure that he was all right. I asked his name and he replied, "Alexander," but then added that I hadn't asked him his middle name. When I did, he answered "The Great." I liked the kid right away.

He stuck close to me until I finally had to tell him that I was working and couldn't play with him. He looked disappointed. I found another chair and brought it to the parents' table. I got some paper and some crayons and asked my new friend to sit down at his parents' table for a while. He was so cute and did exactly what I asked. The parents gave me a dirty look, but since they were not in my station, I didn't care.

Alexander the Great kept watching me and I gave him nods and waves all through the evening. I think he enjoyed himself. I don't know if his parents enjoyed our restaurant that night, but strangely they haven't been back.

GOOD MEMORY

I was working at a new job and learning about my co-workers. It was a nice restaurant and my boss seemed conscientious and comfortable with the customers. He startled me one night when he appeared fixated on a particular diner, one of my customers who was wearing a unique cowboy hat. The hat was black with a silver and turquoise band. The boss called me over and asked what the man had ordered and I told him the beef stroganoff. He then said excitedly, "That's him!"

Thumbing through a drawer full of papers and receipts, the boss pulled out an old one. It was one of our guest checks for two beef stroganoff dinners. The penciled-in date showed it was almost six years old. The boss explained that the same man, with the same hat, had come in and left without paying. He told me he wasn't too worried at the time because he knew the customer would be back and here he was!

I was astonished, and thought to myself, "What a memory, but how is this going to be handled?" Staying out of any fracas, I let the boss handle the situation. Still wearing his hat, the man finished his dinner, paid his check and headed out the door. My boss met him outside and calmly asked if he had enjoyed his dinner. The man said he had. Then the boss asked if he had ever been there before. Why, yes, said the customer, although it had been many years. "And you had beef stroganoff the last time you were here?" The man looked a bit surprised and answered that indeed he had! Then the boss pulled out the old check and casually reminded the customer what day it had been and that he had forgotten to pay. This was done in such a genteel manner, that the customer apologized profusely, and paid up.

Rudeness Stifled

This is a story of how I once stood up for myself at work. A bowling club was having its annual awards dinner at our restaurant. The drinks were plentiful beforehand and when it came time to sit down and eat, everybody was hungry and maybe just a bit impatient.

A banquet menu had been set up for the large group of fifty people. One loud guy gave me a hard time about the menu choices. He was the last to order and couldn't find anything he wanted. His complaints and questions about special requests were holding up the dinner. All his friends were urging him to be reasonable and to be a little less obnoxious with me, reminding him that I was just the waitress and was not responsible for the menu for the night. But he wasn't listening and just got ruder and more insistent.

I finally said quietly, but loud enough for the room to hear, "It is never in your best interest to be rude to your waitress." I was able to finally take his order, but then went outside for a few minutes to cool off so I wouldn't say anything that I would regret. Through the open window, I heard the whole party turn on the loudmouth, scolding him for making me mad and possibly holding up their dinner.

When I finally returned with bread and the first course, tranquility prevailed. The rest of the night went off without a hitch and I realized that a soft word can sometimes be more persuasive than an angry outburst.

RACCOON VISIT

My customers called me to their table late one night because, outside their window, a large raccoon was climbing down a tree branch, just inches away. The dark furry animal crossed along the windowsill, peered back at us, and continued on her way. About the same time the next night, the raccoon climbed down the tree and traversed the same path again. As this was getting to be a nightly routine, I told the customers jokingly that it was our pet.

The restaurant owner was not sympathetic. He went looking for its nest and discovered a hole in the eaves of his building. He told me that he was going to wait and not do anything about the raccoon for a while because she probably had babies in there and she would be difficult to remove. The raccoon appeared in the dining room window regularly for a few weeks.

The spectacle of a big raccoon outside a restaurant window is something of a conversation piece. I used to tell customers about her routine and made jokes about its escaping from the stew pot in the kitchen. Other servers made unsavory comments about raccoon fricasse, and confit of raccoon. Unaware of these possibilities, the mother raccoon brazenly ignored us and went about her business of raising her brood.

Then one night the raccoon brought her babies out with her, and some customers and I went outside to watch discreetly. This was what the owner was waiting for. After the little family was out of sight, he got a ladder, hosed out and then plastered up the hole, putting some steel wool over the repair to prevent the animals from chewing or digging back in. After that, I missed having the animal parade every night, but no property owner wants a family of raccoons nesting in the attic. I was impressed with his eviction method: the raccoons weren't hurt or cooked up, just nudged to move along.

WHY WALTER?

I still can't believe this really happened, but I assure you it did. As usual, I was joking around with my customers, but this time my joke backfired.

We've all heard the expression, "This has your name on it," which means it's meant for you. Usually I describe what dish I've brought to my customers: here's the lamb chops you ordered, with our famous scalloped potatoes, or this is the special duck with pepper sauce. But on one occasion, I put down a dish of salmon pasta in front of my customer and said "This one has your name on it. It says Walter." Why I chose Walter, I can't tell you. In thinking back, I may have heard it with the reservation, but as far as I remember, I just thought Walter sounded funny.

As it turns out, the customer who ordered the pasta was a nice man named Walter. He was dining with his wife, but I don't recall what she had ordered because of the problem that quickly ensued. As soon as I said, "It says Walter," the wife started yelling, "How does she know your name? You told me you have never been here before!" Uh oh! I thought to myself, what have I done?

Walter was stunned. He had no explanation for how I knew his name. I had no explanation for how I knew his name. There was no consoling his wife. Each time I attempted to say that I had just made a joke, it got worse, and she was getting madder and madder. The evening went by very slowly and uncomfortably. I can only imagine the ride home.

The poor man had done nothing wrong! Needless to say, I don't use that phrase anymore. I hope she reads this someday and realizes the truth of the situation, although I still don't understand how I knew his name.

SAVING THE DAY, IF NOT THE HAIRDO

Votive candles add atmosphere to a dining room, making everything appear warm and inviting. We like to use them, especially in winter. But they can be very dangerous.

Two couples were having dinner at one of my tables. As I was standing in front of them, taking the order, one of the women looked for her purse and realized it had fallen under the table. As she leaned forward to reach down for it, her large bouffant hairdo came precariously close to the flame of the little candle and immediately caught fire.

I have heard that hairspray is extremely flammable but I was surprised at how quickly this lady's hair started burning. I took the folded napkin I carry over my arm and used it to pat her hair to put out the flames. At first, she was not aware of why I was patting her on the head. But the terrible smell of burning hair soon filled the room.

To my surprise, she didn't panic and calmly excused herself to go to the ladies' room, probably to assess the damage and recover from such a startling experience. Her hair was singed on one side, but repairable. She had not been burned, which was a blessing, and all four customers were very grateful for my quick thinking in an emergency. I retreated to the kitchen and poured myself a much deserved glass of wine.

CHAPTER SIX

SELECT CLIENTELE

"...in a restaurant, we women act like ladies."

"SIT DOWN!"

One morning I found a new way to handle a very rude customer who was in a rush. He wanted to be served immediately even though the restaurant was busy and full of customers who had arrived before him and were waiting for their breakfasts. He demanded his food loudly a few times, and then got up to leave and said that he was going down the street to another establishment.

I had been very patient with him up until then but decided I'd had enough. When he threatened to leave, I said loudly and forcefully, "Now you just sit right down and be patient. Your breakfast will be right up. If you leave now, you're going to have to drive the car down the road, find a parking space, go inside to sit at a table and wait 'til the server takes your order. Then, you're going to have to wait for them to cook it. Since we're already cooking your breakfast, you're ahead of the game if you stay here!"

He was taken aback, then calmed down and took his seat. I served him breakfast and he stayed for a long time enjoying his meal. As a matter of fact, he was there for a couple of hours, so I decided to talk to him. All I had to ask was where he was from, and we got involved in a long conversation about the ranch he owned and all his animals. He had pictures of his family that he showed me. He had been feeling down and lonely when he came in, but we were friends when he left.

BEING PARTICULAR

Besides being picky about their food, there are other ways customers can be particular. One lady was being very impatient and demanding, asking for many complicated items, starting with a particular way she wanted her hot tea. She listed what I should bring her, in what order and how to serve the requested items. She took many minutes making sure I understood all her instructions.

As I walked away, it dawned on me that her husband had never said a word during the entire encounter and I did not know what he wanted for his dinner. I made a U-turn back to their table and calmly asked him "And are you eating tonight?" He and I have laughed about this since, although his wife did not get the joke.

A TRUE ROMANCE

One of my favorite couples, Ed and Bette Hageman, recently came to the restaurant to celebrate both their 71st wedding anniversary and his 96th birthday. I've known them over thirty years. It's a pleasure to see a couple still together, giving all of us hope for true romance.

We were reminiscing about events that had happened in the past. I recalled one particular time when Ed was having a business lunch/meeting with a client. He is a renowned architect, having built many prestigious homes and buildings. This time his client was a gorgeous blonde and they were sitting in a booth at our restaurant in clear view of all the patrons.

Most everybody knew each other there that day. The architects were at one table, the insurance salesmen at another, the car dealers were in a group, and the judges and lawyers from the Marin County Civic Center were eating and conferring. This was in the 1980s and most of our customers had been in business in the area for many years. We were used to folks having meetings and gatherings for lunch, and many business deals were sealed over a glass of wine and the special of the day.

Ed was building a custom home for the pretty lady.

They had finished with the major design and were fine-tuning the details over lunch. Ed was turning on his considerable charm, probably discussing marble counter-tops and walk-in closets. Unknown to Ed, his wife Bette showed up to join them for lunch. She stood next to the booth, listening to the conversation, behind her husband so that everybody except Ed could see her. She waited for a few minutes, not wanting to interrupt the meeting.

I remember that when she finally did announce her presence, Ed seemed startled. Everybody laughed. It was very good-natured, as we all knew the strength of the Hageman marriage, and only laughed at the idea that a wife would catch her husband "charming" another woman.

Years later, when Bette was describing the event, she told me that she did not want to embarrass her husband. She had stood behind him, waiting patiently for a pause in the conversation and had even thought about leaving as she could hear that the business meeting was ongoing, but decided that she was hungry and wanted lunch. How she got his attention was characteristic of their relationship. She slapped him playfully on his head and said, "Hi, big boy!"

They told me their years together were sustained by a good sense of humor, understanding and listening to each other. We've all heard these axioms, but in their case it's really the truth. In honor of his 96th year, the whole restaurant sang him a heartfelt Happy Birthday, and for both of them, wonderful anniversary wishes. Ed and Bette raised their glasses of wine in happy acknowledgment.

SHE'S NO ANGEL

One of my customers was a beautiful woman named Angel who exuded poise and style. I saw her once in a well-tailored hunter green skirt and matching jacket that reminded me of an afternoon at the polo match, or the horse races. She was married with two sons and appeared to have everything under control. Not only did I admire her, I wanted to be her. From my point of view she seemed to have a life of leisure and fulfillment.

At the restaurant, she ordered dinner but rarely ate it, so I usually had to pack up her meal to take home. I guess you don't keep a slim figure like that by cleaning your plate. When she visited the restaurant, she was always busy conversing with her family, so I didn't speak with her very much except for the usual pleasantries. I just admired her from afar.

One evening she forgot to take her To Go box home with her. When everybody left, there was her dinner, perfectly packed like I had done many times before, but forgotten on the table. I knew the family's last name and found their number in the phone book. When I called, Angel answered. I explained who I was and said I would keep her dinner refrigerated if she wanted to return for it.

First she surprised me by asking if I liked the entree she had ordered. Then she made my day by telling me that I could have it! I was thrilled! It wasn't so much the meal itself, although I think it was Filet Mignon, it was special because this was Angel's dinner and she had given it to me. I took the meal home, heated it up and enjoyed being Angel for a moment, although only vicariously through her dinner.

A few months after that, I was working a lunch shift at another restaurant when Angel's husband came in with another woman for a seemingly romantic meal. Since my manager knew this man, I ran into the back office and told him that Angel's husband was at Table #12, and not with his wife! The manager told me that they had just

gone through a nasty divorce, and the judge in the case had awarded him full custody of the kids. What a sad thing to hear. Apparently I'm a terrible judge of character and my impression of Angel was totally wrong. My Angel was no angel.

I think of this situation whenever I'm feeling envious of others and I've learned to be grateful for what I have and who I am.

WHO COULD THAT BE?

On a quiet evening in the restaurant, there were two women sitting at a booth in the bar area, having a cocktail before going in for dinner. Along with them were a group of regular patrons enjoying each other's company. After the two women went into the dining room, a conversation ensued. There was a lot of going back and forth, until I heard the guys say, "Linda will know."

The topic of conversation was whether or not one of the women was the actress Cindy Williams, famous for her role in *American Graffiti*, filmed here locally. She also played Shirley on TV's *Laverne and Shirley*. Apparently I'm not that good with faces, thought it was not Cindy, and said so. A wager was placed: five dollars to whomever was right.

I was conscripted to go to the table and interrupt the women. "Excuse me," I said, "but I wonder if you could settle a bar bet." They were very friendly. I told them the bet was that she was the famous Cindy Williams. She smiled and quietly nodded that they were right. I sheepishly went back to the bar and put my five dollars down. I had lost the bet.

A while later, when Cindy and her friend were leaving, she came to me, handed me something, telling me that she was happy to have been recognized after all these years. It was five dollars.

AUTHOR TO AUTHOR

I find it hard to call myself an author, because I've been a waitress for so many years. I wrote a little book of short stories *If These Tables Could Talk* but don't like to compare myself to those who have written and made it a profession. When asked, are you an author? I usually respond that I've written a book, but I'm a waitress.

One of my favorite authors is Frank Herbert who wrote the Dune series. The first in the series, *Dune*, is considered to be one of the best-selling science fiction books ever written. I've read it three times. Frank passed away in the '80s, but his son Brian picked up the thread and has continued with an extensive series of prequels and sequels expanding his father's original ideas. I had heard of the new books but did not have an interest, because I enjoyed the original so much. Sort of like the second edition of your favorite movie, it rarely lives up to your expectations.

I was outside of my home a few years back talking to one of my neighbors. He asked if I knew of the Dune series and said that his sister was married to Brian Herbert. Brian had written a biography of his father's life telling the story of how *Dune* came to be written. I was interested and soon had a signed copy of *Dreamer of Dune*. The writing was so captivating that I couldn't put the book down. Not only did I enjoy the story of the background of my favorite author, but now I wanted to read more of Brian's writing. As it happened, we had one of the prequels to *Dune*, entitled *The Butlerian Jihad,* in our home library, but for some reason neither one of us had picked it up and started it. I finished it in a few days, and went looking for the other novels. I now have nine in my possession.

Recently, I received a phone call from my neighbor who said that Brian and his wife Jan were in town. They were all going to come to the restaurant where I work and

Brian had agreed to sign his books for me at that time.

I think I surprised everybody by bringing all nine hardback books. Between the courses, and before I brought him his Rack of Lamb, Brian graciously and personally inscribed each one. I presented him with a copy of my little book of memoirs. After perusing it a bit, he very kindly said that I wrote well. I took that as an extreme compliment, coming from a professional author to a waitress/author.

ANOTHER FAMOUS FACE

There was a familiarity about a new customer. He had warm dancing eyes, and a big dark mustache. It was Phil Frank, the cartoonist from the San Francisco Chronicle. I recognized him from his comic strip Farley because he drew the main character as a caricature of himself. I loved his cartoon depictions of the bears of Yellowstone Park named Hilda and Alphonse. I asked him, "Are you Phil Frank?" He smiled and said yes. I don't like to bother my customers while they're trying to have a nice meal, so didn't talk to him much other than to say that I looked forward to his daily cartoon.

I was very pleasantly surprised when he left me this drawing on the placemat.

PARENTING?

Some unruly children were making a lot of noise and commotion in the restaurant, dashing among the tables, almost colliding with the servers and refusing to sit down.

The parents were just sitting there and offering no guidance at all. We were all wondering how this could be happening when we heard the parents say to the kids, "Don't they teach you any manners in school?"

EARLY MORNING ENERGY

One morning, a family with three kids was pretty quiet when they arrived at the restaurant for breakfast. Then Mom and Dad had their coffee, and the kids were plied with hot chocolates made by me. I make them very chocolatey, the way I like it, with lots of whipped cream. The children were also treated to pancakes, shaped like Mickey Mouse with fruity condiments for the mouth and eyes. Plenty of syrup was poured on top.

The sugar and caffeine was taking effect as the kids started laughing and having fun. Dad was in on the excitement and encouraging the playtime at the table. He was the one who started running around the table to play hide-and-seek. Other customers were not appreciating all the commotion, as it was their morning, too, but nobody was complaining. It was rather nice to see the family having so much fun with each other.

As one couple was leaving, they stopped at the family's table. The man mockingly said to the father, "Do I have to come over here to calm things down?" It was said in such a friendly way that everyone laughed. The couple explained that they had raised their own family and remembered when their kids had gotten a little out of hand at the table, but weren't used to Dad being the instigator.

It was one of those mornings in the restaurant, with such a fun atmosphere, where all the customers left with a good feeling in their stomachs from the food and a good feeling in their hearts from the family at play.

SIT UP, PLEASE

I had an unusual request from one of my customers. A woman, dining with her daughter and granddaughter, asked to speak to me discreetly. She whispered that they were there that evening to teach the young girl how to sit properly and eat in a restaurant. The woman went on to explain that she wanted me to participate in the learning adventure.

I listened and was wondering what I could possibly say to someone else's child. Things got more interesting when the grandmother told me to tell the little girl that there was a special table set aside for children who did not behave properly while in a restaurant. My immediate thought was that I would scare the poor child if I told her something like that, and she would be afraid of me, and perhaps of all servers afterwards.

I put the request in the back of my mind, not sure of how to handle the situation, and proceeded to wait on the table as I normally would. I took extra care in taking the little girl's order, speaking to her directly about her pasta, asking her if she wanted it with only butter or with some added tomato sauce. I tried to put her at ease and she smiled at me. The three women shared some soup to start, and I was relieved that everything was going smoothly.

After a little while, I brought the pasta, as well as the other orders and everyone started eating. I understand that it is hard for a young person, with lots of energy and a short attention span to sit quietly for a long time. Soon the little girl was squirming in her seat, sitting sideways, leaning on her mother, and then started to run her hands along the wood grain of the wall in a play-like fashion. The grandmother glared at me, as if to say, "Tell her to stop doing that!"

I moved behind the little girl, and spoke to her quietly. I straightened her chair and told her that while you're in a restaurant, you sit up straight like a lady. As I pushed her chair in, I playfully rocked it back and forth, and told her it was like a Disneyland ride going right up to the table. Then I pointed to another table of six adults and showed the little girl how everyone was sitting straight and speaking softly to each other. I explained to her that children can run around when they're on a playground, but in a restaurant, we women act like ladies.

She was so excited that I was taking time with her; I could tell she was really listening. This conversation was just between me and my new young friend. I did not want her to think that I was in collusion with her mother or grandmother, or my little lesson might not have gotten through to her.

I explained to the other waiter what was happening at the table. He informed me that while he watched, the little girl sat up very straight each time I approached them or walked by. She was trying, and it was very heartwarming. She got chocolate ice cream for dessert because she had been so good. On the way out, she stopped in front of me and smiled a big grin, with a chocolate smudge on her face. I asked her name, and she said, Charlotte. I thought it was a beautiful name for a young lady.

I still don't think it is my job to train the young ones who come into the restaurant, but I was happy to help Charlotte, and I think she'll remember me.

FAITH

One of my customers is a truly spiritual as well as religious person. So I thought she would appreciate the following religious joke that I had recently heard:

A man was in a flood and as his house began to fill with water, so he climbed up onto his roof. A neighbor came by with a rowboat and told him to jump in. The man said, "No, God will take care of me."

The water continued to rise, and the sheriff came by in a speedboat and told the man to jump in. Again he answered, "No, God will take care of me."

Finally when it looked like the whole house was going under, a helicopter swooped down, but the man still refused, repeating that God would take care of him.

Then he drowned and went to see St. Peter. The man complained that God was supposed to have taken care of him, and St. Peter answered, "We sent you two boats and a helicopter!"

I saw my customer a few weeks after that, and she came up to me and said, "You were the one who told me that joke about the drowning man and the boats and helicopter, right?" I said that I was. She apparently had gone directly to her brother to tell him the joke. It pertained to him because he works on the San Francisco Bay on boats and tugs.

My customer explained that twice her brother has had close calls with boats capsizing and his having to be rescued from the bay. They were scary incidents, but turned out not to be too serious. She told him the joke and ended with, "When God sends you a helicopter, get on it!"

Then one Saturday there was a very bad storm. My customer's brother and his captain had gone out past the Golden Gate into the Pacific to salvage an abandoned boat. They caught sight of the floating wreck, but the seas had become too high to retrieve it and they decided to come back to shore and try again another day. They did not make it back. Their boat capsized and the captain was lost. My customer's brother was rescued by a helicopter. He was rushed to the hospital, suffering from severe dehydration and shock. He will recover, but is extremely sad at the loss of his friend, the captain.

I had heard on the news that a boat had gone missing that day, and knew of the incident when my customer rushed into the restaurant to tell me that it was her brother's boat that had gotten into trouble. She came specifically to thank me for telling her the joke so that she was able to tell her brother to get onto the helicopter. As she wisely explained, "Coincidence is God's way of staying anonymous."

IN MEMORIAM

Besides bringing their own bottles of wine to a restaurant, customers often bring in decorations or centerpieces for their tables. Flowers, candles, and balloons usually, but sometimes unique items to celebrate a particular event. The extra effort can personalize the table and make any gathering feel more like a celebration at home.

Packaged glitter and confetti available at party stores can be festive, but it is hard to clean up afterwards. On one New Year's Eve celebration the confetti left the dining room in such a mess that my customers left extra tip money "for the poor guy" who had to vacuum the next day. Such thoughtfulness is rare.

I'll never forget the time a beautifully carved box was

brought in and lovingly placed in the center of a round table for the six family members there having lunch. They explained to me that their Auntie had recently died and her remains were in the box. The aunt had been too sick to come out to lunch with them in the last few months of her life. They conversed with her as if she were there and even ordered a strawberry dessert with hazelnut that had been her favorite selection. When the lunch was over, they took her with them when they left, and no extra vacuuming was necessary.

FAIRNESS OR FAVORITISM?

Our restaurant provided helium balloons for the children. They were colorful, bouncy and popular with the kids. If there was more than one child, I always made sure to bring all the same color. This was to be fair and prevent any fighting or crying over a preferred color. I did this to keep the peace.

However, when I wanted to stir things up and cause some mischief, I brought one ice cream dessert noticeably larger than the others.

CHAPTER SEVEN

IN THE BAR

"Don't smell it, don't taste it, just drink it."

One Night in the Saloon

A family arrived at the restaurant one evening, a couple with a little girl who was about six years old. As the hostess started to escort them to their table, the couple looked around and did not see their little one with them. They asked where the girl might have gone off to and I answered, "Don't worry. She's at the bar."

The little girl had gone right up to the bar, found an empty stool and hoisted herself up. I watched her, thinking that her parents had also seen her. She was so cute and apparently determined, that nobody stopped her. She put both elbows up onto the counter and sternly said to the bartender, "Whiskey!"

After the laughter died down, Dad explained that the family had been watching John Wayne movies on the television that afternoon.

Cheers!

Before you enjoy a glass of wine or a cocktail with a friend, the glasses are often touched together for good luck and there is a distinctive clink. Roger, my French Basque boss told me the reason for the tradition. A glass of wine should have all the senses associated with it. Sight, smell, taste and touch are obvious. The "clink" provides the fifth sense: sound.

The Art of Bartending

My new job required me to be a bartender. I stepped up with confidence, as I've watched bartenders pour and serve for many years. I even know most of the ingredients. I soon found out that it is not as easy as it appears.

Almost anyone can mix up a drink or two especially an easy one like gin and tonic. It's just gin with tonic, right? But the proportion is very important and can make the difference between an excellent cocktail and a poor one. The bartender also has to take into consideration the fact that alcohol affects some folks' behavior and can change their moods, sometimes dramatically.

At first I thought I was doing my customers a favor by pouring a strong drink, but as it turns out, moderation is the way to go. One patron stayed with me at the bar most of the evening, having four drinks over a period of more than four hours. He later commented that he felt too inebriated when he left because of "the way you were pouring them!" I thought he was a seasoned bar patron and knew what he was doing, but learned from that comment that the object is not to pour a strong drink each time, but to moderate the intake ever so discreetly. That is the art to bartending.

On another occasion, a patron asked for a double while he was waiting for someone to join him for dinner. He finished it rather quickly and asked for another, which I provided. He paid for the drinks with a hundred dollar bill.

About twenty minutes later he asked for one more double. I told him that I did not feel comfortable giving him another drink so quickly, and that I would wait until his dining partner arrived. He became quite rude, demanding that I give him his drink, implying that I had cheated him on the first two. He pointed his finger at me and said loudly, "Let's make sure we're on the same page," but I did not give in. Although he initially told me that he was waiting for his friend, he got up and left the bar. I was thankful that he had already paid, and I was glad to see him go. It was time for my break and another bartender came on duty.

When I returned from my dinner break, half an hour later, I noticed the same man at the bar having what appeared to be a double shot. He had waited for me to go off the floor to come back in. I had not warned my fellow bartender about him as I thought he had left. When he saw me, he finished his drink and went out the door. Good, I thought, I did not want to have another confrontation.

A few minutes later he apparently returned with a woman to have dinner. I did not see him come in as he was in the restaurant part of our establishment and not in the bar area. He was being deliberately stealthy. They were seated at a table and he ordered his drink, a double, from his waitress who put the order into the bar. I poured the drink not knowing that it was going to be served to a man who had already had his limit.

Initially I had given him two doubles, the next bartender had given him another, and now he had finished his eighth shot of booze within an hour. We servers are supposed to confer with each other to prevent such an occurrence, but this man had outwitted us. The accumulation of alcohol took its toll, and he slumped in his chair, too drunk to sit up or eat. As it turned out, the friend that he was waiting for was his wife, who proceeded to yell at us for serving him too much. Their evening was ruined as she helped him into the car to get him home.

I learned two lessons that day; first, to be very careful of the power of alcohol and its control over some folks, and second, why the rule for servers to confer with each other about consumption is so critical. I felt sorry for the wife who had a bigger problem on her hands than us serving him too many drinks.

BEER AND BREAD

A German friend once told me that beer is often referred to as liquid bread, both made with the same ingredients but in a different form. He then explained that if you have a beer for breakfast, this is understandable. Continuing on, he cautioned that a man who has a shot of whiskey in the morning; well, he has a problem.

MEN AND THEIR WIVES

The man at the bar was sitting quietly, enjoying a beer. He was just one of the many patrons who were there spending the afternoon watching television and chatting. It was an ordinary day at our neighborhood watering hole.

The front door flew open, filling the place with a burst of sunlight from outside. An obviously angry woman came storming in and went straight for her husband, the quiet man having a beer. She started hitting him on his back and head with her big white patent leather purse, yelling that she had told him never to come in here. We all felt sorry for him as he sheepishly got off his stool and left with her.

A few days later, another neighbor came in and started piling dimes, nickels and pennies on the bar counter. He carefully counted out a couple of dollars worth of change and asked for a beer. As he kept looking over his shoulder, he explained that his wife had given him only enough money to go to the store for some dog food. She was afraid that if he had any left over, he would spend it at the bar!

Besides the large parking lot in front of the restaurant, there was extra parking space behind the building. I used to joke that the pick-up trucks were parked there to avoid being seen by passing traffic. Now I knew better, it was to avoid being seen by passing wives.

WATER AND VODKA

I was teasing my customers one day as I refilled their water glasses for the third or fourth time (apparently they were very thirsty) by stating, "Here's more vodka!" My silly comment opened up a whole conversation on liquor and what would happen if it really had been vodka they were drinking.

I told them about a customer of mine from many years ago who had a regular order of seven double vodkas with dinner. His instructions were that the drinks should be brought to the table in a tall water glass so as not to be recognizable as cocktails. He must have realized that 14 vodkas was an exorbitant amount to drink. Strangely enough, I never saw a difference in his behavior in the course of the evening. We held nice conversations and there was no slurring of words or clumsiness. He just had a tolerance for that amount of alcohol.

Then one day he surprised me by ordering an iced tea, which was his wife's drink of choice. His explanation was that he had quit drinking for a while.

The sobriety lasted for about a month. One night this same couple came to the restaurant for dinner and I asked if they were both going to be having iced tea. He told me to bring him his usual drink: the doubles disguised as a tall drink of water. He ordered them one after the other and I brought them because I knew him and thought he could handle it. However, the month of abstinence had remarkably lowered his tolerance.

Soon, my customer was slumped over in

his chair, passed out. His wife did not bat an eye, simply reached for her phone and dialed. Within a few minutes, their two large, strapping sons arrived, picked Dad up, one on each side and carried him out. The wife left a substantial tip for me, assuring me that he would be all right. I'm not sure if the gentleman continued his vodka habit at home but he certainly didn't drink to excess anymore at the restaurant.

WATER AND VODKA AGAIN

When I finished telling my water-drinking customers the story, they responded with a water and vodka story of their own. One day a friend of theirs rang their doorbell, pushed open the door and ran through the house stripping off his clothes. He knew the house and proceeded straight through to their backyard and jumped into the pool.

As their now-naked, swimming, laughing friend paddled around their pool, my customers realized they had another problem. Their good buddy worked for a lumber service and drove a large truck, which he had precariously parked only halfway up their driveway and it was partially blocking the road.

They called the man's wife who said she had been trying to contact him for a few hours and was wondering where he was. Apparently, about every three years, the lumberman falls off the wagon in a dramatic way.

Both stories were entertaining, and illustrated two different instances of mixing water and vodka in unusual ways.

WINE EXPERTISE

Selecting a bottle of wine in a restaurant can be simple or complicated, depending on the customer. Some folks don't know that much about the offerings, and will pick out a bottle as if they were choosing a horse in a race: whatever name sounds interesting. Some select on the price alone: either the cheap ones or the expensive bottles, chosen only for their assumed superiority.

I was in Georgia a few years ago, and saw a nice bottle of California wine listed for a very good price. I guess I impressed my dining companions by asking, "How much for the Stephen Vincent?" I might have sounded a bit pompous. It was offered at only two dollars more than the house selection, and is a quality wine. We ordered it and it was excellent, as I'm sure were most of the others on the list, but the familiarity of the name led me to choose it.

Another time I traveled to Italy with my mother, sisters and sister-in-law. We had many delicious lunches and dinners. I instructed my family to order the house wines when we were in restaurants in the small towns. One benefit of house wines in Italy, besides the fact that they were all delicious, was that the labels had the name of the village. They were colorful and distinctive, providing a memento of where we had dined.

I took the different bottles back to our hotel each night and soaked the labels off to keep in my scrapbook as a souvenir of our visit. I soon figured out that the bidets in our hotel rooms held the bottles perfectly, soaking them horizontally so that the label peeled off nicely in one piece the next day. My mother made us all laugh when we were at breakfast and she proclaimed, "There's a different bottle in there every morning!"

Just a Show Off

When I returned from my vacation in Italy, I waited on a gentleman well-dressed in a nice suit and expensive shoes. He had a cocky, know-it-all attitude mentioning that he was familiar with restaurants all over the world. Asking to see the wine list, he perused the choices only a short time before he handed the menu back to me. He pronounced that there was nothing on the list for him. He was quite rude, adding, "There's nothing good here!"

Feeling intimidated, I went into the kitchen to speak to the chef, an educated European with real experience in restaurants all around the world. The chef calmly told me that the customer was full of hot air and there was no way he could possibly be familiar with all of our wines. I realized then that the gentleman was just a show off and so was able to ignore his pompous attitude and serve him as professionally as I knew how.

THE BEST RED WINE

A couple of businessmen came in one day and immediately ordered our most expensive bottle of wine. It was a 1995 *Duhart Milon Rothschild*, priced at $150. Most of our other wines are in the $25 to $60 range. The owner overheard the request and immediately went to the cellar to retrieve the bottle, as it was kept under lock and key.

I stayed at the table to finish taking the order. Only seconds later, my boss appeared with the coveted bottle. It was slightly dusty on one side, a good sign that it had been stored properly. I noticed that he brought three glasses with him even though there were only two customers at the table. He made a deal with the customers that he would open the bottle and take the first taste. If it was still good, they could not send it back. The businessmen agreed. The wine was opened carefully, so that the delicate cork

would not break off and fall into the bottle. The boss took a small sip, pronounced that it had held its character, and the wine was poured. There was a little sip left in the taster glass so I also got a small taste of the costly stuff.

As I later told a friend, it was the best red wine I'd ever had. However, for me personally, I'd rather go with a more reasonably priced label and save the extra money for a new pair of shoes.

SHY AND LOVESICK

One customer was known about town for being a social drinker. I saw him regularly at our bar. He was outgoing and friendly with everybody, often being the life of the party.

He was apparently interested in one of the waitresses at our restaurant. He quietly asked me one night if I thought he had a chance with her. I don't like to get involved with such personal questions and told him to ask her himself. He must have really fallen for her because I saw him watching everything she did, although he never approached her. I hadn't realized that he was shy because of his conviviality, but this was different. This was personal and a matter of the heart; we all have insecurities in that area.

Then one night, this gentleman was acting very drunk. He approached me and leaned against a wall as if he couldn't hold himself up. He was slurring his words, but managed to convey that he wanted me to give him the waitress' phone number. I am usually reluctant to do that and hesitated, although I had her number memorized. As I paused and considered my answer, the "drunk" guy slumped a little more and slid down the wall, his shoulder hitting a small light switch and turning it off. This light switch was for an outdoor light that went dark. The inside hallway where we were talking remained lit. He could not have seen the outside light from where he was slumped against the wall.

The "drunk" guy realized what he had done, pushed his shoulder back up and turned the light back on. I knew then that he was just pretending to be inebriated. There was no way that someone as drunk as he was acting would have noticed hitting a small switch like that. I realized that he was hiding behind the alcohol to protect himself from rejection. All this went through my mind for a split second as my psychology studies from college came rushing back to me. I decided to stay out of the whole situation, made an excuse and walked away.

My shy customer ultimately asked the waitress out and she accepted. They went on a few dates, but it never got serious. It was a learning experience for me, how some folks are so confident on the outside, yet remain quite personally vulnerable.

THE PIED PIPER ROOM

A famous watering hole at the Palace Hotel in San Francisco is the Pied Piper Room. When I worked there several years ago, I dressed in my elegant Gunne Sax gown and served drinks to sophisticated businessmen and couples. At that time, the lighting was subdued, the wallpaper dark green plaid and the chairs around the small cocktail tables were upholstered in red leather, creating the ambience of an exclusive men's club. The room got its name from the large oil painting, *The Pied Piper* by Maxfield Parrish, hanging behind the bar above the many tiers of liquor bottles.

The afternoon and early evening cocktail hours were good shifts to work. Important lawyers, executives and newspapermen from the *San Francisco Chronicle* stopped there for an hour of socializing after a long day.

I came to work one day with an upset stomach. The bartender told me to take a shot of a *digestif* called *Fernet Branca*. He admonished me, "Don't smell it, don't taste it, just drink it." I trusted him and downed the dark stuff. A nice warming started in my esophagus even before it hit my stomach and suddenly I was cured!

Fernet (we're now on a first name basis) has been made in Milan, Italy since 1845. It is a tincture of 29 herbs, including mint, licorice and dandelion root and doesn't taste good. In fact, it tastes a little like dirt. The bartender was correct when he told me to "just drink it" or I might not have gotten the whole dose down.

Traveling a short distance up Montgomery Street from the Palace Hotel brings you into North Beach, the section of San Francisco settled by Italian immigrants, so Fernet was a popular request at the bar. Older Italians remember their mothers giving it to them in small amounts when they were children.

A friend was in the restaurant a while back. He does not drink alcohol, just never acquired a taste, so he says. His stomach was acting up so I suggested a shot of my "medicine." I told him that even though Fernet was alcoholic, it would do him good. He took the drink and immediately wrinkled up his face with distaste. He looked like an unhappy little boy, which amused me. I went to his table about fifteen minutes later and asked him how he felt. He said, "Oh, I forgot about my stomach." I call that testimonial a Fernet success story.

The drink is a very old recipe and it fit right in with the historical setting of the Palace Hotel and the men's club atmosphere of the Pied Piper Room. I am grateful to the bartender who introduced me to my favorite cocktail, settling my stomach and giving me a lesson in history at the same time.

CORKAGE

Corkage is a curious thing. The customer pays to bring his own wine to a restaurant that is in business to sell wine. Some of the earliest comments I ever heard on the subject have stayed with me.

One restaurant manager said, "Pretty soon they'll bring a bag lunch and want to sit at one of our tables!" But the most memorable response to "May we bring in our own wine?" was, and always will be, "I don't bring my girlfriend to the Mustang Ranch!"

At one restaurant, a large celebration was planned and the customers arrived with three cases of wine, all pre-opened. An arrangement had been made for the corkage fee of so many dollars per bottle opened up at the event. I guess they did not realize the fee is to compensate the restaurateur for the money lost by not selling beverages to their party. They had uncorked all 36 bottles of wine before they arrived hoping to avoid the fee. As it happened, not all the wine was consumed and many opened bottles, now ruined, were carried back home. The good part of this story is that the restaurant only charged corkage on the number of empty bottles.

There are times when the fee is waived. Winemakers sometimes bring their own vintages and give a bottle or two to the owner. This is considered a professional courtesy and no cork-age fee is charged. I recently waited on a table of eight wine brokers who brought and opened up a dozen bottles of wine to taste and compare.

Their table was conspicuous with so many bottles opened, and brought up questions from the other diners. I explained that they only tasted a small amount of each and hoped they would leave the remains in the bottles for us servers. They did, and at the end of the night we tasted, actually finished, each one.

The worst corkage occasion for me as a waitress happened a few years ago. I was waiting on a couple who were celebrating their tenth anniversary. They brought a nice bottle of French wine, given to them by their parents on their wedding day for this particular anniversary. I carefully uncorked the bottle, gave them the required "taste", and proceeded to pour. Something happened, I'm not sure what, but the bottle slipped from my hands and shattered on the floor.

This is one of those times when you want to crawl under a rock. There was no getting around what I had done. I told my boss what had happened and he was very sympathetic. He actually went to his own personal collection and served the couple a very nice bottle of French wine. He had saved the occasion for the customer and never asked me to pay for it. The couple was understanding and said at least they had a "taste" so they could tell their parents that they liked it. A corkage fee was naturally not charged at that table.

THREE FOR THE PRICE OF ONE

By serving Sunday brunches over the years, I have become accustomed to the brunch drinks of choice, most notably mimosas (champagne mixed with orange juice), and Ramos Fizzes, which I call an adult milkshake. I have a reputation for mixing a very good Ramos Fizz, made with gin, an egg, heavy cream and orange flower water. I got the recipe from a former co-worker of mine who used to make them three at a time in a big blender behind the bar.

I was watching him mix his concoction one morning in front of a customer who had ordered one. He put in plenty of heavy cream, two eggs, gin, orange flower water for the required taste, and a touch of triple sec. He carefully poured one serving for the patron who drank it very quickly and stuck his empty glass out for more. The bartender was surprised at the speedy gulp of such a heavy drink and asked the customer if he wanted another so soon.

Apparently, the customer expected to get the whole amount, saying that it was customary to empty the contents of the blender. In the instance of an ounce and a half martini or Cosmopolitan, it is customary to empty the contents of a shaker. But this time was different as there were three portions of Ramos Fizz. The bartender seemed stunned and did not speak for a  second, and the impatient customer repeated with emphasis, that it was customary!

Feeling that there was conflict ahead, I explained to the customer that the bartender had mixed three portions in the same shaker because he had other orders. The unhappy patron left the bar with some disappointment. The bartender had made him a very good drink but he had not enjoyed it because he had gulped it down in anticipation of getting three for the price of one.

HUMOROUS DRINKING TALE

Despite some of the problems I've encountered with overconsumption, including some personal experience, I can still joke about it.

There's a story about a man who customarily ordered and drank three drinks, one for himself and one each for his brother and father in the old country. One day he only ordered two, and the bartender remarked that he hoped everything was okay, asking if maybe something happened to his brother or his father. The man responded that no, it was himself he was leaving out, as he had been drinking too much.

Taking Your Work Home

I used to work with a bartender who told me that he works eight hours during the day, then works another eight hours at night. He was referring to his dreams, and told me that his brain did not shut off, so he thought about pouring drinks all night long.

The same thing has happened to me. Especially after a particularly tough shift, I have awakened in the middle of the night, thinking I'm at work, serving tables in bizarre situations. In one dream, the number of people in my station doubled each time I entered the dining room. Another time, I went into the kitchen and was suddenly outside. There was no kitchen, and I woke up worrying about how I was going to get the iced teas that had been ordered. One time, I was home in the shower after work and suddenly remembered, "Oh yeah, she wanted mayonnaise."

It would be better to leave it all behind when we aren't working, but that's hard to do sometimes. I'd like to believe it's because we care about the work we do and our customers. The personal contact that we make, when we provide a good meal and friendship, carries over into our own lives.

This is all well and good, but does not explain one waitress nightmare I had where I was in a bathtub with Chef Ed, a frothy, bubble bath with both of us fully clothed. I mentioned it in the kitchen the next day, because the theory is, if you tell your dream, it won't come true. So far, so good.

CHAPTER EIGHT

MANY HALLOWEENS

"Then the Wicked Witch charged in wearing a spectacularly realistic costume, complete with a fire-shooting broom!"

HALLOWEEN AT WORK

Halloween used to be just for kids. Not anymore. It's becoming more and more of an adult holiday, where we can be who we really are. I have a theory that Halloween brings out secrets of our personality. What this says about me remains to be seen.

One restaurant where I worked for a number of years had a costume policy: if you worked on Halloween, you must be in an appropriate costume. If you did not want to participate, then you got the day off. I always volunteered to work on this festive holiday. Now came the fun part: what should I wear? Who or what could I be for the day? The possibilities were endless! Since I worked at this restaurant for more than a decade, I had the opportunity to come up with some interesting costumes.

For my first year, I decided on a scary costume: a full mask of a realistic-looking skull. This was a mistake, since I could not converse with the customers. To make it worse, one of the cooks told me that if he could not hear me, he would not put my food up. This was somewhat true, but come on...let's get with the spirit of the holiday! I ended up taking my mask off early on, and found my hair all messed up. I learned a lesson that day: no full masks.

The rest of my costume was just a black Danskin leotard with a scarf around my neck. The look was dark and minimal, since I thought the skull itself was sufficient. All in all, this was not a successful Halloween outfit. When I first arrived in said attire, the chef told me to go back home and put some clothes on. Although, as you can see by the picture, I did not comply.

A few of the memorable costumes worn by my co-workers were a very, well executed Wonder Woman complete with the figure to pull it off, and a pretty lady who dressed up as a devil with red paint on her face. Nobody recognized her for a few minutes. The red paint changed her features.

Our lady bartender Mary Ellen, did a tremendous job as Mae West one year, and we waitresses wore T-shirts from brothels of Nevada to be her "girls" for the night. The T-shirts were a gift from a customer who visited a few of the sporting houses in Reno. We made a pact to wear them on Halloween.

One clever guy did not have a costume to wear for the day, so he put his waiter uniform on backwards with the tie hanging down his back. It was simple and effective giving the illusion of his head on backwards.

It's always fun to see what people come up with as popular characters and movies come to life this time every year. Perhaps the costumes let us become what we want to be, or are scared of...or just to be silly for a day. What a great holiday!

GOING POSTAL

Another year and another Halloween costume, which I really enjoyed, was a "crazed postal worker." This was when the post office was having shootings. Not a very funny subject, but I thought, macabre enough to spoof on such a holiday. I bought some ill-fitting postal pants, grey with a black stripe down the outside of each leg from a second-hand store and made some patches for a light blue shirt. Some googly-eyed glasses helped with the crazy effect.

I carried three guns: a rubber band gun, a cap gun and

an efficient water pistol. These three were confiscated from me right away. (Aww...) The costume got a lot of attention. I thought my idea was unique, but another waitress wore almost the same thing, although she was not appropriately armed.

TOOL TIME

The next year, I had to step things up since I was getting a reputation for creative costumes. At the time, the TV show *Home Improvement*, with Tim Allen, was popular. The actress playing Heidi, the Tool Time Girl, had a large bosom. I decided to dress up as Heidi but needed a little help in the bosom department. I started asking around for a large bra that could be stuffed for the occasion. Some of my customers have a clubhouse nearby, and they told me that there was a 44DD red lace bra that had been hanging in their clubhouse for a few years. Nobody was sure where it had come from, or who originally lost it, but it was their property now and I could borrow it for Halloween,

Well, that bra did a very nice job as Heidi, with me and a pound of cotton. I was dressed very comfortably in hiking shorts, hiking boots, a khaki blouse opened to show off the red lace bra, and a borrowed tool belt. To complete the outfit, besides the enormous bosom, I had made a sign for my back that had to do with tools and drinks. The sign said: Tool Box Drink Specials: Screwdriver, Rusty Nail, Wallbanger, with pictures of corresponding tools, 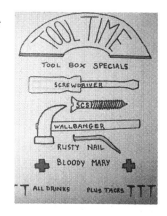 and all drink prices included "tacks." I thought it was very clever.

THE DOG CATCHER

Since I like to recycle some of the costumes, the next year I turned my postal cap into an official-looking dog-catcher. I copied a nice picture of a golden lab, and pasted it onto my cap. Then I attached four or five stuffed animals to last year's postal outfit. I had one around my neck (like the poor thing was holding on) one on my back and a few on my legs and arms. I bought these stuffed dogs at my favorite second-hand store and apparently didn't look at them too carefully because one little girl commented to her mother, "Look, it's a Christmas dog!" True, one of the little stuffed animals had a Christmas ribbon around its neck. I distributed the dogs to the kids who came to the restaurant that night which made it fun for everyone.

THE BIG RED BRA

The bra was such a hit that it reappeared the following year. I dressed up as an Artesian, from a TV ad for Olympia Beer. Not only did the bra come into play for this dress-up, I painted myself blue with Halloween make-up. I discovered that body makeup was not a good thing to wear for a five-hour shift, working with food. Plus the paint made customers ask if I was a Smurf...that hurt.

The commercial went something like this: the beer is made by Artesians, a fictional people who are invisible. A popular joke circulating at the time explained that Artesians can't be seen, but you can find them in women's bras because their little noses stick out. I augmented the concept by stitching little blinking Christmas lights into the huge, overstuffed bra to indicate the presence of the Artesians. This was in the days before LEDs and I had a small battery pack with an on/off switch. I approached my tables as a costumed waitress, I threw the "on" switch, and my "can't miss 'em" boobs lit up!

My costume was a big hit. During the lunch rush, my on/off switch broke and the chef was kind enough to stop work and fix it for me. I realized then that the kitchen workers appreciated my costume because nobody minded the delay while the chef helped me.

After my costume mistakes with the mask, the paint and the malfunctioning light switch, I simplified the subsequent outfits by making sure they were comfortable to work in. The costumed atmosphere was a draw for the restaurant, and we were always busy on Halloween nights.

THE KING OF HALLOWEEN

A restaurant manager I worked with for many years loved Halloween and decorated the restaurant with spooky scenarios using dolls, werewolves, flying witches and a small, model haunted house with a sound system and steam blower for effect. One year he had an automated model of the famous shower scene from Hitchcock's *Psycho* set up, backlit as a silhouette behind a shower curtain. This was definitely a realistic and scary effect. He was acquiring a reputation for being the King of Halloween.

A few weeks before the holiday, he and his friends wove a large spider web out of twine to encase the front door, with a gigantic stuffed spider laying in wait. Even though it was make-believe, I did not like that spider and web, so I used the back door for the whole month of October.

On Halloween night he usually had a magnificent costume, but one particular year he decided to dress up his whole family as the characters of *The Wizard of Oz*. They had walked in the town parade earlier in the day and won first place for creativity and excellent execution. My manager dressed as the Wicked Witch. His beautiful wife was in a fully detailed ball gown as Glinda, the Good Witch. Their son dressed as the Tin Man, with the heads of the Scarecrow and the Lion attached to his costume. Their little girl was Dorothy with a basket and a little stuffed dog.

At about 7 PM, the restaurant was bustling and busy with costumed patrons and servers when there was a big scream. Everybody turned and looked as the front door of the restaurant burst open. Glinda ran in with the costumed children and yelled out that they were hiding from the witch. They ran around the restaurant, ducking in and around the tables, getting everyone's attention. Then the Wicked Witch charged in wearing a spectacularly realistic costume, complete with a fire-shooting broom! The restaurant erupted into applause and I commented to a few nearby customers, "That's just our manager coming to work."

THE BIG RED BRA LIVES ON

I had opened a can of worms with my Halloween costumes. Each year, I had to outdo the previous year's rebirth of the famous red lace bra. I wore that bra for the next six or seven Halloweens in a different style each year, most of the time with an assortment of ever more sophisticated blinking lights. The bra was outrageous, but nobody got offended because the size was so cartoonish. The poor thing is all worn out now because of all the times I had to over-stuff and fit it with safety pins.

It never did get back to the clubhouse, although I was told there was a picture of me wearing it on the wall. When

I went to look, I found a close-up picture of "the bra" tacked to the wall. Frankly, it could have been anybody in the picture because there was no face or body shown. But we all knew that it was me, and as I said before, a pound of cotton. The last few years, I wore the lit, stuffed bra under a bright orange blouse, and called myself a 'blinking pumpkin'. This was somewhat subdued compared to the old days. My friend  was sweet when she said to me, "You're too skinny to be a pumpkin. You're a squash!" I believe the old lace bra has had its day and is now retired.

POPEYE'S LADY

One year, I dressed up as Olive Oyl from the Popeye cartoon. I made an acceptable Olive Oyl, again with comfortable boots to work in. I handmade a black skirt with red trim and a large turtleneck sweater. I pulled my hair back and had a bun sticking out just like I remembered from the cartoon. The Mexican cooks in the kitchen called out, "Olivia!" and understood my costume right away. My friends and customers thought my depiction of Olive Oyl was OK, but wanted the big bra back. I had established a reputation for making the bra come to life.

PUNNING IN FUN

This image needs clarification. Watching late night TV evokes strange ideas, especially when it's *The Howard Stern Show* around Halloween time.

One night Howard Stern, the ultimate juvenile, had a woman parading around in her thong underwear on his TV show. As I was watching, I happened to notice a pair of flip flops on my living room floor. This sparked an idea for an interesting Halloween costume.

When the time came for me to go to work, I put on a neutral Danskin outfit, adorning it with a deflated bicycle tube wrapped around my bosom, and a flip flop dangling down my backside. I told everyone my costume was entitled, "A Tube Top and a Thong."

It was fun to wear, but needed some explaining to my co-workers and customers, as you can imagine, especially those who don't watch Howard Stern.

HALLOWEEN REMEMBERED

While I was writing these stories, I wondered if they would be interesting to my readers. So what if I had worn different Halloween costumes? I stopped writing since it was time to go to work, but kept the question in the back of my mind.

That night I waited on a family that I hadn't seen for a long time. I learned that the mother had passed away and the dad had been through an illness soon after. Dad and daughter were at the restaurant reminiscing about the old days, saying it was good to be back in a place where the family had such nice memories.

Out of the blue, the daughter mentioned how her Mom had always enjoyed my Halloween costumes, especially the ones with the blinking lights. She told me that her mother had been in an early state of dementia at the time and couldn't speak well, but was always cheerful. When I came to the table with the electronics going, she would smile, nod her head and blink her eyes along with the lights. The dad told me that they talked about it on the way home, asking her if she saw the lights, and could she believe such a costume! She had giggled and seemed to appreciate my sense of humor. It was one of the stronger memories they had of their mother. It felt good knowing that my costumes had brightened someone's life.

CHAPTER NINE

OUT AND ABOUT

"...traffic lights and pedestrian crosswalks provide
a certain pulse to the passing parade..."

THE CROOKEDEST STREET

There is a main artery heading north out of San Francisco as a pathway to the Golden Gate called Lombard Street. The thoroughfare starts out as 'The Crookedest Street' high atop one of San Francisco's famous hills, descending with switchbacks to accommodate the vertical nature of the terrain. On busy days, there is a constant stream of cars, often with a waiting line, enjoying the fun of traversing the course. I've driven down Lombard Street myself, as a daytime activity.

For nighttime fun, Lombard Street has other stories to tell, and the tales concern naked people...three different times!

Lombard is very heavily traveled. The timed traffic lights and pedestrian crosswalks provide a certain pulse to the passing parade of transit buses, tour buses, delivery trucks and autos. The street is lined with motels, apartment buildings and many choices of eating establishments, so there is always a heavy flow of pedestrians, day and night.

Early one morning about 1:00 AM, Thor and I were standing on one of Lombard's many busy corners, waiting for the bus home and watching the scene.

Sitting at what seemed to be a very long red light just in front of us, was a small dark BMW coupe with wraparound windows. Calmly seated on the passenger side was a naked woman, not ten feet away from us. I was delighted to see something out of the ordinary, and discreetly got Thor's attention. He was able to get a quick glimpse of the woman in all her glory before the coupe sped away. Lombard Street had not disappointed. Our evening out had included some quirkiness, good clean fun and a story to tell.

NAKED AGAIN: THIS TIME IN A RESTAURANT

Over the years, I've visited many of the restaurants on Lombard. There used to be a good German place, famous for its delicious strudel, and a '50s-style café with burgers and shakes. But for some reason, we usually ended up at Clown Alley, a nondescript chain restaurant with decent hamburgers, chili and American fare.

Situated at the far north end of the street, it was a last stop for a lot of folks on their way home to the North Bay and the 24-hour format of the place made it a haven for characters. My friend and I decided to have a bite before leaving the city, again about 1:00 AM. Of course it had to be me who saw the streaker running along Lombard Street, laughing as he passed by. I had a clear view through the large picture windows of a completely naked man with everything swinging side to side. This did not however interrupt my snack. I made everyone laugh when I called out, "Again?"

Of course I had to tell all the strangers within earshot about the first time I had a naked encounter on Lombard Street. We had a good chuckle together about the continuing saga and that added to the late night camaraderie. Plus I now had another story to tell.

THIRD TIME'S THE CHARM FOR LOMBARD

Months later, you won't believe it, but it happened again. This was another early morning, at the magic hour of 1:00 AM and at Clown Alley again. It wasn't a streaker this time, just some guy casually walking past the picture window carrying his clothes and shoes. No concern for any of us who were trying to enjoy our food. I took this in stride and just held my hands up in disbelief. No conversations with any of the other diners. Nakedness had become commonplace on Lombard Street.

We moved north shortly after that and don't go into San Francisco as often for late night entertainment. Lombard Street still pulses and flows, but Clown Alley is no longer there. An era has come to an end. I never thought I'd miss Clown Alley.

JUST DESSERTS

Be careful of how you treat your waitress. You may see her on the outside. I was waiting on a table of four, consisting of two couples. I don't remember how the trouble started, but our rapport never gelled. Apparently they thought that I was misunderstanding their order and one of the guys at the table seemed to be particularly dense when I was trying to explain some of the dishes. We were not getting along very well and he became quite rude with me. It was not a good feeling, and I'm sure the party did not enjoy the evening because of the tension. In retrospect, I should have called another waitress to take over the table, but for some reason I stuck it out until the very end, trying at least to be professional.

The event bothered me because I usually get along with my customers. It stayed on my mind so I easily recognized the same man a few weeks later in a store in my hometown. I was shopping for antiques. In front of me at the counter was my rude customer. He had a basket full of items and was paying for them. Although the prices were clearly marked, he dickered on each piece, "Will you take two dollars?" "How about only fifty cents for this one?"

This went on for some minutes. I could hear the entire conversation as I waited patiently behind him to pay for my one six-dollar item. Soon there were other folks forming a line. Finally, after all the bartering had been settled, he had a pile of purchases on the counter and some small tables and furniture all now belonging to him. Without hesitation, he asked the shopkeeper if there was a van to deliver the goods, since there was no way it would all fit into his Porsche. This reminded me of an appropriate joke.

I admit I was a bit perturbed by having to wait for him all that time in line, listening to that complaining voice again. For some reason, I was not afraid to butt in and add my two cents. You see, here I was a private citizen and he was on my turf. I had shopped at that store many times and was friendly with the owner. My run-in with this guy previously had been limited by my employment at the restaurant, where I couldn't really talk back. Here was my chance!

From behind the Porsche owner, I spoke up and casually asked the storekeeper if he knew the difference between a cactus and a Porsche?
My former customer then turned around to face me and hear the end of the joke, when I said, "The cactus has the prick on the outside." Everybody in line (there were quite a few of us by then) laughed. But he wasn't amused. He then recognized me as the waitress from the restaurant, pointed his finger, saying loudly and with a touch of anger, "You!"

I was embarrassed and surprised at my candor, so I quickly put my money for my purchase on the counter and left. I know that I should be careful about insulting people, but his actions in the store and in the restaurant warranted a fitting response. I have to admit that I felt vindicated.

LATE NIGHT AT DENNY'S

I must have been drinking a bit or perhaps I would not have overreacted about something as simple as scrambled eggs. It was 2:00 AM and I specifically wanted some perfectly fluffy scrambled eggs before we went home after a night out. Denny's restaurants have an "Always Open" motto and being situated across from the CHP station in Corte Madera means activity at all hours of the day and night. Thor and I stopped in one night. He ordered a chicken sandwich and I theatrically explained to our waiter how I wanted my scrambled eggs to be light, fluffy and steamy. Our waiter gave us a slightly annoyed look.

From where we were sitting, we had a clear view of the open kitchen and I soon saw our order placed on the counter under the heat lamps, ready to be served. I saw the chicken sandwich with the french fries and my scrambled eggs with the wheat toast. The eggs looked fabulous. I could see them steaming and hot, looking quite delicious.

Our waiter came out of the kitchen, looked at the plates, looked at his order book, flipped through the pages and then went back into the kitchen. I heaved a huge sigh of disappointment. I wanted my eggs to be served while they were still hot. Our waiter appeared again, looked at our plates, thumbed through his order book again, this time glancing around the dining room. I wanted to yell out, "Over here!" but for some reason restrained myself. The waiter retreated back into the kitchen. I kept my eyes on my eggs. They were no longer steaming.

However, I was starting to steam. I told Thor that I was perfectly capable of getting up and serving our order myself. He didn't think that was a good idea, what if it wasn't our order? I said

that it was somebody's order, and it was getting cold!

The third time our waiter appeared, he spotted me glaring at him, and like a light bulb turning on, realization came over his face. He picked up the forlorn dishes and brought them to our table.

I immediately sent back my eggs, sternly reiterating that they needed to be fresh, hot, steamy and fluffy. I finally got served after Thor finished his sandwich. My eggs were OK, but the charm of the establishment and my enthusiasm had worn off. In the car on the way home, we agreed that we would no longer sit where I could see the kitchen.

DESTINY?

Working in San Francisco meant commuting on the bus. My ride home was late in the evening after the dinner shift. I soon got to know most of the regular bus riders. One of these was a Japanese woman who I discovered was also a waitress at a restaurant in Japantown. We started to sit together regularly and chat about our jobs. We waitresses can always find something in common, and commiserated with each other about our bosses, co-workers and customers.

I visited her at her restaurant and enjoyed the sashimi, sesame spinach and gyoza, Japanese pot stickers. The eel was fantastic served in a small enameled box with rice. When my sister came to visit, I took her there and her small son peeled off all the breading of the tempura and ate only the shrimps and vegetables that were underneath. My sister and I both thought he was  probably smarter than we were, not eating all the carbs.

My friend and I spent many an hour on the bus, and besides work, we discussed life. We talked about our experiences, our different takes on situations and our philosophies. We spoke of destiny, fate or karma, whatever you want to call it. One of her biggest beliefs was that you choose your situation in life, even your parents and the time you are born. Her idea was farfetched as far as I was concerned, because when she saw a person having difficulties, such as homelessness or a crippling disease, she would tell me that in some way they had chosen that lifestyle.

In January of 1982 Marin County was hit with a big rainstorm and corresponding high tides. We had a county-wide flood and many places were inundated, including our house. The county was paralyzed for a day.

There are many famous photos of rivers of water running through city streets that day. My Japanese friend lived in San Rafael on the Miracle Mile heading out to San Anselmo, in a three-story apartment building with a parrot as a roommate. There were three fatalities due to the flooding that day, and my friend was one of them. Her apartment house slid down the hill in a mudslide. The other occupants were not home because they worked in the daytime, but she worked at night and was asleep in her bed when the mud came through. Her parrot was saved because he was hanging from the ceiling in his cage. He was adopted by one of her neighbors.

I cannot ask my friend now, but I can't help but wonder about her take on the situation. Would she appreciate the irony? Did she "choose" to be there at that time? It is a question that has haunted me since. After all it was her philosophy about which we had many discussions. This is just one of those strange unanswered questions of life.

I WENT TO A GARDEN PARTY

I am a good waitress and apparently presentable, so I'm often asked to do private parties on the side. The extra income is always welcome so I usually accept. Most events are enjoyable and very lucrative. But private parties are all different so you learn to go with the flow, depending on the circumstances. One in particular, I'll never forget.

I took the bus into the city, was met by a limousine and driven to an estate in Atherton, a very affluent community down the peninsula from San Francisco, with large spacious homes and grounds. On the way, I looked out of the limousine windows, enjoying the view and wondering about the folks who lived there. Wearing my standard black skirt and fancy white blouse, I hoped that I was dressed appropriately and would be acceptable in this venue.

The car turned into a long driveway with a gorgeous home at the end. There was a large back yard surrounded by trees, gardens and a pool. This event was to be a political fundraiser. Out on the lawn I helped set up the tables and chairs, and then added tablecloths and centerpieces. Caterers brought the sumptuous spread of appetizers. There were lots of bottles, more booze than food, I noticed. The party was to start at noon, and be over by three o'clock.

Guests began to arrive and I steered them to the festivities. Everybody was dressed up in elegant clothes, but very nice and relaxed. A gentleman approached me, asked my name and conversed with me as an equal, which made me feel like an invited guest. This was not acceptable to the

hostess. She hustled right over to us and informed the man that I was the help and not part of the party. I was put in my place and afterwards kept to myself doing my job of keeping everything clean and organized. I'm good at that anyway, whether I'm being paid or not.

As the drinks flowed, the conversation and laughter intensified. Everyone was having a good time. The pool looked quite inviting, especially to me as a swimmer. I thought that if I were to attend a party like this, I would want to bring a bathing suit to enjoy the whole atmosphere. Apparently there were no such restrictions on this group. Who needs a bathing suit? One woman who was wearing a white linen sheath dove right into the pool, dress and all. There was a great roar of approval as she emerged from the water revealing the fact that underwear was optional.

As three o'clock neared, I was told that the hostess needed to take her afternoon nap and that the guests should be asked to leave. How could I do that? I was told to start folding up the chairs and bring them into the house. Most of the guests were still sitting in them. I literally took chairs away from underneath people, explaining that the hostess wanted the party to end, and got very dirty looks from folks who had intended to stay a while. Word got around quickly that the party was over.

I was paid a few hundred dollars, a tidy sum and well worth the experience. The limousine dropped me off on Van Ness Avenue to wait for my bus home. I was once again among the ordinary people going about their daily business. With the dreamlike quality of the past few hours now fading into memory, it became just another day at work.

As I waited for the bus, I had time to think about this party and the other interesting experiences I've had over the years in my line of work, meeting many people, seeing different venues and lifestyles. Then I felt the money in my pocket, smiled and caught the next bus home.

CHAPTER TEN
AND IN CONCLUSION...

"Serve the food promptly, making sure everybody has the correct entree."

As my stories show, I am able to recall many wonderful and unusual things that have happened in restaurants. Although I may joke around and tell tales, I actually take my work as a waitress very seriously and have trained many young folks in the art of service. I like to stick to common sense rules of cleanliness, promptness and consideration. Here are the guidelines that I share with any new waitstaff:

Linda's Guidelines: How To Turn The Tables
Greeting Your Customers
The server should have a greeting ready to say, something short and sweet like:
>Hello, good morning (afternoon, evening)
>It's nice to see you again
>Thank you for stopping in today

By having a prepared statement, the server is not pressuring the guests to immediately respond. Sometimes the customers want to chat, and there is a time and place for that, but sometimes they are just hungry and thirsty, not looking for a lengthy conversation when they first sit down.

Show your knowledge of the menu; take pride in what the menu offers:
>The soup is terrific today: It's tomato bisque and I think you'll enjoy it.
>The chef has prepared a delicious special; our famous fish tacos made with crispy Icelandic cod, served with a salad for $9.95.

Followed quickly with:
>What may I get for you while you're looking at our menu?
>Would you like something to start? Coffee, soda, or perhaps a Bloody Mary?

A shrimp cocktail is just the thing to begin your dinner. The shrimp look extra large and fresh today.

The trick here is to suggest something. It's not enough to ask if anybody wants a drink...let them know what is good in this particular restaurant by enthusiastically describing one or more of the house specialty drinks. It is not so important what is offered, within reason. It does not matter if the server personally enjoys any of the suggestions, only that they provide an idea of what is available.

Taking The Order

This is the most important part of your job. Tell the customers about any specials not listed on the menu. Listen carefully to their questions and requests. Be as helpful and accommodating as possible. This is where the server can suggest and guide the guests to selections that will be satisfying.

Once they have told you what they want, be sure that you have a clear understanding of their order. Ask questions if you need clarification.

Have fun. Act as if you are at a party, enthusiastically discussing the food that will be served.

After The Table Has Ordered

Do not ignore the party. Now is not the time to return to personal conversations at the coffee machine.

Be available. Stand in the dining room in full view of the tables. The customers may need an extra napkin, or a spoon for their coffee. Pay attention.

Serve the food promptly, making sure everybody has the

correct entree. Check for any drink reorders. Verify that the guests have any special knives or forks they might need for their entree.

Now you can demonstrate the art of "checking on the table." Within a few minutes, walk by and look around the table. Does everyone seem happy with their choices? A good server can tell by body language if things are going well.

Never interrupt the meal to ask if everything is okay. First of all, we want it to be better than okay, and it won't be okay if the server rudely interrupts the conversation. Quietly ascertain the needs of the table.

Are the guests looking around in need of something?

Has the server forgotten anything, particularly any extras that were requested?

Again, paying attention and being available are the most important attributes of a good server.

Clearing The Table
It is the server's responsibility to "weed" their tables. Just as you would weed a garden of any unwanted plants, a good server removes the empty plates and utensils as soon as they are no longer being used.

Etiquette dictates that the server should not start clearing the dinner dishes before everyone has finished, so that the customer who is eating a bit more slowly doesn't feel rushed. However, there are exceptions to this rule. Sometimes diners want their plates removed, or in the case of a banquet with many people, it is acceptable to start clearing as the plates are emptied. The table should always look neat and ready for the next course.

When The Entree Is Through

Offer dessert, bringing menus so the customers will know what is available. Make suggestions:

> You might enjoy the caramel apple crisp or the brownie sliders.

Offer coffee, or suggest Espresso with a dessert wine.

Bring the check in a timely manner. Guests do not want to have to wait to pay their bill once the meal is done.

If the transaction is in cash, without question, bring the exact change required. A tip is always voluntary, never assumed unless previously arranged, as with a banquet.

Thank your customers. They have many other options for a meal out, and we want them to know that they are appreciated.

Now, go to work and have fun!

Made in the USA
San Bernardino, CA
17 January 2019